F. C. PAVILO

ROME IN COLOUR

ALBUM AND GUIDE

THE VATICAN
THE SIXTINE CHAPEL

CASA EDITRICE LOZZI · ROMA

GENERAL INDEX

LEADING EVENTS ROMAN HISTORY

Rome is situated 41°, 53' 52" N. lat.; 12°, 28' 40" E. long., on the banks of the Tiber 14 miles from its present mouth.

The 21st of April 753 B.C. is regarded as the day of the foundation of Rome.

When first founded Rome was governed by Kings (753-510 B.C.): afterwards as a Republic by Consuls (510-27 B.C.), and lastly by Emperors. During the 8th century it became independent under the Popes and it remained the seat of the Papal Court till the 20th Sept. 1870, when the Italian Government entered Rome and the Eternal City became the Capital of United Italy.

The Vatican, a little territory occupied by St. Peter's Basilica and Square and by the Vatican Palaces, is under the Sovereignty of the Pope, and has assumed the name of Vatican City State.

The population of Rome is about two millions and half.

There are more than 400 churches. The major Basilicas are seven: St. Peter's in the Vatican, St. Mary Major, St. Lawrence outside the Walls, St. John's in the Lateran, St. Paul outside the walls, Holy Cross in Jerusalem, St. Sebastian on the Via Appia.

* * *

The Kings of Rome. 753 B.C. Romulus murdered by the Senators; 718, Numa Pompilius; 673, Tullus Hostilius; 640, Ancus Martius; 616, Tarquinius Priscus; 578, Servius Tullius; 534, Tarquinius Superbus (the Proud).

667. Romans and Albans contesting for superiority agree to choose three champions on each side to decide the question. The three Horatii, Roman knights, overcome the three Curiatii, Alban knights, and unite Alba to Rome.

509. Tarquin the Proud and his family expelled for tyranny and licentiousness: royalty abolished: the Patricians establish an aristocratic commonwealth.

Republic. First period (510-87 B.C.) from the expulsion of Tarquin to the Dictatorship of Sulla. — Second period (87-30 B.C.) from Sulla to Augustus.

496. The Latins and the Tarquins declare war against the Republic and are defeated at Lake Regillus.

477-396. Wars with Veii and the Etruscans. Veii taken by Camillus after ten years' siege.

390. Great victory of the Gauls near the Allia. They sack Rome, a disaster which threatened to alter the course of history in Italy: they accept a heavy ransom. Rome is gradually rebuilt but great distress and wars with neighbouring States. Samnite wars.

312-308. Appius Claudius, Censor, favours the lower classes: makes the road from Rome to Capua called the Appian Way, and erects the first acqueduct. Rome supreme in Italy.

264. Punic Wars. 146. Carthage destroyed. 63. The Catiline conspiracy. 48. Pompey defeated at Pharsalia. Caesar, who in every sphere of life attained the highest excellence as a politician, an orator, a general, and a man of letters, on the 15th March 44 B.C. is assassinated at a meeting of the Senate.

42. Battle of Philippi: Brutus and Cassius defeated. 31. Anthony totally defeated at Actium.

The Empire. 27 Octavianus becomes Emperor under the name of Augustus Caesar. Rome now at peace with all the world. The Temple of Janus shut. Jesus Christ born. The Empire at the apex of its greatness. Augustus' reign coincides with the golden age of Latin literature. In this century the voices of Cicero, creator and master of Roman style, and of Virgil, the representative poet of Rome, resound in the Eternal City. Moreover, there are: Horace, the greatest satirist of Rome; Tibullus, the most refined and tender of elegiac poets; Propertius, the « Roman Callimachus »; Ovid, the most facile and brilliant of the elegiac poets; Livy, in whose great historical work the record of national life receives its most systematic exposition; Tacitus, the last powerful voice of Rome, and many others.

14. A.D. Tiberius. 37. Caligula. 41. Claudius. 54. Nero.

61. St. Paul sees Rome for the first time, in January 61 A.D. entering the city by the old Porta Capena: visits Rome for the second time in 66 and after a long term of imprisonment is beheaded at the Aquae Salviae on June 29th, in 67 or 68 A.D. On the same day St. Peter, the first Pope, is crucified head downwards.

64. Under Nero the city is burnt down and the crime is blamed on the Christians.

68. Galba, Otho, Vitellius. 69. Vespasian.

70. Jerusalem levelled to the ground by Titus. Colosseum built by Vespasian.

79. Titus. 81. Domitian. 96. Nerva. 98. Trajan.

117-138. During the reign of Hadrian, Rome attains its greatest pitch of architectural splendour and although some magnificent structures were erected after this time, we must on the whole, date from this period the decline of the City.

138. Antoninius Pius. 161. Marcus Aurelius. 180. Commodus. 193. Septimius Severus. 211. Caracalla.

270. Aurelian begins the enormous task of making the city defensible by building the Walls.

283. The Forum is seriously damaged or completely destroyed by the great fire of Carinus.

284. Diocletian and Maximian.

312. Constantine the Great, as the result of a vision, places the cross on his banners and favours the Christians.

331. He removes the seat of the Empire from Rome to Byzantium. On his deathbed he receives baptism at Nicomedia.

361. Julian, the Apostate, abjures Christianity and reopens the heathen temples; he is killed in battle in Persia.

379. Theodosius. 395. Honorius.

404. Rome placed under the exarchate of Ravenna. Distress of the provinces. Invasion of the Barbarians. The City at her lowest state.

410. Rome is sacked by the Goths.

475. Romulus Augustulus, the last Roman Emperor.

476. Odoacer, king of the Heruli, puts an end to the Roman Empire of West.

493. The Goths establish their reign in Italy.

553. The Byzantines expel the Goths from Italy, which returns under the Emperors of the East.

568. The Lombards invade Italy.

572. Stephen II: under this Pope the temporal power of the Church commences.

800. A.D. Charlemagne crowned Emperor of the Holy Roman Empire of the West by Pope Leo III on Christmas Day.

1073-1085. Gregory VII (Hildebrand), vigorous reformer, opposes Henry IV respecting investitures.

1084. Robert Guiscard lays waste the entire southern quarter of the City from the Forum to the Lateran. Strongholds erected on the ruins of monuments of antiquity.

1300. Boniface VIII proclaims the first Jubilee.

1305. Clement V removes the papal seat from Rome to Avignon.

1347. Cola di Rienzo, the last of the Tribunes, establishes a Republic; assassinated in 1354.

1370. Gregory XI protector of learning, restores the papal chair to Rome.

1503-1513. Julius II begins the destruction of old St. Peter's, to build the present church; Bramante is called to take the leading part in the great enterprise.

1513-1523. Leo X, son of Lorenzo il Magnifico, made Rome the centre of culture. A period of the most glowing splendour and reckless magnificence succeded the sterner rule of Julius II.

1523-1533. Clement VII refuse to divorce Catherine of Aragon and denounces the marriage of Henry VIII with Anne Boleyn. Beginning of the Reformation. The Imperial invasion of Italy and the Sack of Rome (16th May 1527) ended the Augustan Age of the papal city in a horror of fire and blood.

1585-1590. Sixtus V as a real innovator of the plan of the city, enriches Rome with many new buildings.

1861. On March 27th the Italian Parliament declares Rome to be the natural and indispensable Capital of the new State.

1870. On September 20th the Italian troops entered Rome through the breach of Porta Pia (Pia Gate).

1929. On February 11th Roman question is finally settled by means of the Conciliation between the Church and the Italian State, through the Lateran Treaty which, since the year 1947 has been part of the new Constitution.

1946. On June 2nd Italy becomes a Republic by referendum.

1962-65. Ecumenical Coucil, the 2nd of the Vatican, begun by John XXIII and finished by Paul VI.

The beautiful **CAPITOL SQUARE**, designed by Michelangelo, with the Palazzo Senatorio, head-quarters of the present City Administration.

CAPITOLINE HILL
IMPERIAL FORUM
COLOSSEUM
ROMAN FORUM

We reach the **CAPITOL** by climbing the large flight of stairs, called « Cordonata », designed by Michelangelo and made for the triumphal entry of Charles V in 1536

The bronze statue of **Cola di Rienzo,** is by Masini. It is placed on antique fragments, to show that the last Roman Tribune wanted to re-establish the Republic on the ruins of the Empire. Cola was the son of an innkeeper. By reading the Latin classics as well as he could, he filled his mind with the glory and greatness of Rome: this glory he determined to restore again. The statue was erected in 1887 presumably on the spot where the Tribune was killed by the people. Nearby, an encaged she-wolf — a living symbol of Rome — calls the tourist's interest. At the top of the stairs are the colossal groups of the **Dioscuri,** Castor and Pollux, found near the Ghetto and placed here in 1583 by Gregory XIII. Sixtus V added the **Trophies of Marius** and the **statues of Constantine** and his son **Constantine Caesar.** We now reach **Piazza del Compidoglio,** designed by Michelangelo for the munificent Pope Paul III (1534-1549). The old artist placed on a new pedestal the equestrian statue of **Marcus Aurelius** (161-180), the only one of the many bronze equestrian statues once adorning Rome that has survived The Emperor-philosopher seems to welcome the visitor with profound benevolence And he appears to be so august, so worthy to reign that no one can refuse to render him homage. Here he is not the same Emperor that we see shut in the museums; here he is the man of the Forum and the Capitol: a worthy representative of the Caesars It is common opinion that the preservation of this statue is due to the fact that it was believed to be Constantine, the first Christian Emperor. We may also believe that Alaric and the other barbarians who came afterwards with their ruin and pillage spared this statue because they were impressed by its air of superb magnificence and unlimited authority. The statue was never in the Forum, in front of the Arch of Septimius Severus, as was supposed. It was at the Lateran, in the house of Verus, descendant of Marcus Aurelius, whence Michelangelo removed it in 1538. It was gilded; and the people believe that when the gilding of the horse becomes bright again, the world will end.

The **Palazzo Senatorio** was built on the antique ruins of the Tabularium in the 13th century The present façade is the work of Girolamo Rainaldi according to the design f Giacomo Della Porta. The stairs and fountain are by Michelangelo. Three statues adorn the fountain. the Tiber and the Nile on the sides and Triumphant Roma (of too modest proportions) in the centre. The Senatorial Palace is the residence of the Mayor of Rome.

The **Capitoline Tower** was erected in 1579 by Martino Longh In the time of Constantine a cross was erected on the Capitol: it remained there until the end of the last century, when a Mayor of Rome, during a period of anticlerical hysteria, had this symbol of our civilization removed. On the 4th of November 1924, the same cross, so dear to all true Romans, was again put in its place.

In the Tower there is the famous bell, called « Patarina », ceded in 1200 by the people of Viterbo as the price of peace. For the last seven centuries, this bell has called the Romans to mourn for the death of a Pope, or to enjoy the Carnival Festivities; to crown a poet, or to announce capital punishment; to sign a peace treaty or to declare war; for all the joys and all the sorrows of Rome.

The **Tabularium** was erected by Q. Lutatius Catulus in 78 B.C. The bronze tablets of laws and decrees are kept here. It is one of the few remains of the Republican era. In the 13th century, the Palazzo Senatorio (Senatorial Palace) was built over it.

From the Tabularium we have a glorious view of the most celebrated spot of ancient Rome: stupendous temples, triumphal arches, monuments of every sort.

As we look at the ruins from this height, in our imagination we see the people, the priests businessmen hurrying to the tables of the money-changers, the idlers strolling about discussing or ascending the steps of the immense temples, gossiping. A thousand different scenes rush through our minds, recalling the greatest events of private and public life. According to the well known legend, the battle between Romans and Sabines was fought in this valley after the Rape of the Sabine women; a battle ending almost theatrically with the intervention of the women. Peace was established and the valley between the Palatine and the Quirinal was chosen by the two tribes as a common ground for a market and meeting place: that is the meaning of the word « forum ».

The **CAPITOLINE MUSEUM** contains a rich collection of antique marble statuary.

In the courtyard is the famous statue of **Marforio**, over a fountain. A wide staircase leads to the first floor.

In the centre of the first room, is the **Dying Gaul**, a copy in marble of the bronze statue of the monument of Pergamos; the simple, natural position of the body, the face expressing profound anguish yet full of dignity, all combine to make this one of the most brilliant statues of ancient art. All round the room there are other famous statues, expressions of ideal beauty. The celebrated group of **Cupid and Psyche**, an enchanting Hellenistic creation, represents the chaste kiss of two young lovers. The **Satyr** is the best copy of an original bronze statue by Praxiteles, who had the divine gifts of tender beauty and grace.

Second and third rooms: various sculptured works of art. The fourth, or philosophers' room, contains many busts of Greek and Roman writers and warriors. In the centre, the seated statue is believed to be **M. Claudius Marcellus**, one of the Roman generals of the Second Punic War who, after a long siege, occupied Syracuse. where the famous Greek scientist Archimedes rendered useless the powerful machines of the Romans. Among the many busts, four are of the great epic poet of Greece, **Homer**, who sang the heroes of Troy, and was disputed as citizen by seven cities. Tradition represents him as a poor blind man. **Socrates**, the celebrated Athenian philosopher, is here with his flat nose, thick lips, protruding eyes, like a satyr. Before drinking the fatal poisoned cup, he had already set forth his idea of the immortality of the soul.

The fifth, or room of the Emperors, contains about eighty busts of Roman Emperors and Empresses; it is the most interesting portrait

The bronze EQUESTRIAN STATUE OF MARCUS AURELIUS, the only surviving statue of the many ► that adorned ancient Rome.

gallery in existence. The name of Caesar is commonly given to the first twelve Emperors These who, when we were in school, seemed like myths to us, now become men of yesterday through their life-like busts in this room. Art has made them our contemporaries.

Room of the Doves:

The **mosaic of the Doves** was found in Hadrian's Villa at Tivoli and was at once recognized as the one described by the naturalist Plinius. It might even be taken for a painting, so fine is the work.

In the lovely figure of a **Maiden clasping a Dove to her Breast,** when attacked by a snake, we see a symbol of the human soul making the choice between good and evil.

Room of Venus:

The **Capitoline Venus** was found in the Suburra

A characteristic view of VIA DEI FORI IMPERIALI, seen through two of the Colosseum's arches. The ARCH OF TITUS can be seen on the left against the green background of the PALATINE.

The CAPITOLINE SHE-WOLF is the symbol of Rome. Legend has it that Romulus and Remus, the sons of Mars, were saved and nursed by a she-wolf. Romulus founded Rome on the 21st April in 753 B.C.

in the 17th century. It is perhaps the most pleasing presentation of all the goddesses; here we admire her in all her beauty, full of charm and grace. It is in the style of Praxiteles. The **Palace of the Conservatori** contains innumerable artistic treasures.

The first room was painted by Giuseppe Cesari, Cav. d'Arpino. He worked here for more than forty years. The other rooms were painted by Laurenti, Daniele da Volterra, Caracci, etc. The admirable statue of the **Cavaspina** (Boy extracting a Thorn from his Foot) in the third room, belongs to the pre-Phidian period. It is probably the best surviving statue of that time. In the fourth room, the **She-wolf** is ancient. The She-wolf is an Etruscan work. The two children were added during the Renaissance. The other rooms are full of antiques.

The **Pinacoteca Capitolina,** picture gallery, countains some important masterpieces, among others: Romulus and Remus, by Rubens; Cleopatra and Augustus, by Guercino; The Rape of Europa, by Paolo Veronese; St. Sebastian, by Guido Reni; St. Petronilla, by Guercino; Magdalene, by Tintoretto; portraits by Van Dyck, etc.

S. MARIA D'ARACOELI rises on the highest point of the Capitol, site of the Rock or Citadel of Rome. A legend relates that Augustus raised an altar here to the « Son of God », to recall the oracle of the Sibyl about the coming of the Saviour. This church inherited the glory of the ancient Capitol; it became the national church of the nobility and people of Rome, the principal seat of the medieval Senate, whence the laws of Rome were proclaimed.

The « Capitoline Basilica » is very picturesque with its secular relics, its tombs, its frescoes, its gilded ceiling and ancient trappings. It originally belonged to the Greek monks, then to the Benedictine Fathers till 1250, when it was given to the Franciscans. It is reached by a staircase of 124 steps that was built in 1348 as an offering to the Blessed Virgin for freeing Rome from the pestilence. Cola di Rienzo was the first to climb these steps.

The richly ornamented pulpits at the back of the central nave are by Lorenzo Cosmati and his son Jacob (XIIIth century).

On the left of the transept, the octagonal chapel dedicated to **St. Helena** marks the place of the other altar of the Augustan legend. Right under the altar of St. Helena, at a level 15 cm. (6 in.) lower than the present pavement, there is a white marble altar, embellished with sculpture and mosaic. They illustrate scenes of the above-mentioned legend which can be interpreted with the help of the scenes on the table of the altar. It dates from the 12th century.

In a small chapel in the sacristy, the *Holy Child is kept. A poetic legend narrates that a Franciscan friar who lived in Jerusalem, one day made a statue of the Child Jesus in olive wood. He was sad for he had no colours with which to paint it, but during the night angels came down and painted it for him. The friar brought the statue back with him, the boat sank off the coast of Leghorn and the precious box was lost. But after a few days, it was miraculously washed upon the beach. Thus the good friar was able to bring it to the Aracoeli Church.

During the Christmas festivities, the Child is placed in the artistic crib prepared in the second chapel of the nave, on the left. Roman children go there to recite the traditional « sermons ».

On going out by the main door, we admire the large staircase erected in 1348, the Romanesque façade and a splendid panorama of the city. The **MONUMENT TO VICTOR EMMANUEL II** (or « Vittoriano »), erected as the apotheosis of italian independence, was designed by Count Giuseppe Sacconi. It was begun in 1885 and inaugurated in 1911. It rises at the foot of the Capitol and is late neo-classic in style. In fact, the allegorical groups, the trophies, the columns, the bas-reliefs, works of the best sculptors, return to the ancient Roman style for decoration and splendour. A Venetian sculptor, Chiaradia, worked for twenty years on the equestrian statue of the King. The powerful bas-relief on the base, representing the various ruling cities of Italy of the past, was designed by Maccagnani, who collaborated for years with Sacconi on the plastic decorations. The large bas-relief on the sides of the « Altar of our Fatherland » is by Zanetti. It reminds us that Western Civilization owes its present direction to the impulse given it by Italy. From the remotest times, in every human achievement, Italy gave the world a Master. Literature, art, science, religion, law, all owe Italy a great debt of gratitude.

Under the statue of Roma is the **Tomb of Unknown Soldier**.

Piazza Venezia, the centre of Rome, and therefore of Italy, takes its name from the Palazzo Venezia, built in 1455 by the munificent Venetian Cardinal, afterwards Paul II (1464-1471). It was the finest palace ever seen in Christian Rome, filled with works of art. It is a typical example of the first period of the Renaissance architecture and of the change from castle to palace.

TRAJAN'S FORUM. The Emperor M. Ulpius Traianus was born at Italica, Spain, in A.D. 53. The most formidable undertaking of his reign was the conquest of Dacia. The Dacians had as prince a military genius, Decebalus. Domitian had to accept an ignominious peace and

The BASILICA OF S. MARIA D'ARACOELI and THE CAPITOL.

The inside of Basilica.

for ten years Decebalus prepared an army modelled on the Romans'. Trajan would not bear this humiliation any longer. In 101, he left for the Danube. His first enterprise was to prepare roads and fortifications. The capital of Decebalus was taken and he was forced to terms which he did not keep. In 105, there was another struggle. The Dacians fought desperately: « Victory or Death! », but their army was destroyed. The heroic prince killed himself. Trajan returned to Rome loaded with treasures. After celebrating the triumph, as a monument to his victory he decided to erect a Forum that should surpass all others in size and splendour, under the direction of the great architect, Apollodorus of Damascus. The new Forum became the finest place of the city. There were two libraries, a column of honour, a basilica, a temple, a big equestrian statue of Trajan, a triumphal arch and statues and groups everywhere. Towards the middle of the century the Emperor Constans visited Rome, accompanied by the Persian Prince, Orsmida. When he came to Trajan's Forum, he was so astonished at the stupendous work that he exclaimed: « It would be impossible to imitate

A panoramic view of Rome from the Victor Emmanuel Memorial. VIA DEL CORSO, one of Rome's most central streets joining PIAZZA VENEZIA and Piazza del Popolo, can be seen in the baskground.

The MONUMENT TO VICTOR EMMANUEL II., designed by Sacconi, was erected to celebrate Italian independence.

it; at the most, I could make the horse! » and the Prince replied: « Your Majesty, for a horse like that, you need a stable like this ».
But the great Monument of the Dacian War is the noble column that still rises in its pristinc majesty, bathed in the glory of more than nineteen centuries.
The ashes of the Emperor were placed at the foot of the monument and his statue on top of it. The column consists of 19 blocks of marble and a spirál staircase leads to the top. The most important part of this historic monument is the helicoidal band of figures going all around it which gives us a documentary view of the arms, arts and costumes of both

the Romans and the Dacians. Here we see the bridges Trajan built, the forts he attacked, the camps he destroyed, the enemy he put to flight. The old interpretations of the inscriptions on the column have now been recognized as exact. The column shows how deep an excavation was dug to make room for the Ulpia Basilica. This is also shown by the writings of Dion Cassius, who says that the ground was hilly and uneven and Trajan had it levelled even with the top of the column
The large complex aggregat on of edifices called the **Trajan Markets,** has been completely brough g g o ps   o er formed by a semicircle o hree oo   ell

preserved, and an upper, containing a large vaulted hall, called « Basilica Traiani ». These buildings are admirable for their archeological value and for the fine architectural proportions. The **FORUM OF JULIUS CAESAR** was built with the spoils of his Gallic wars. On the 9th of August 48 B.C., the decisive battle was fought between the formidable armies of Pompey and Caesar. The Julian Family boasted its origin from Julius, commonly called Ascanius, son of Aeneas, born of Anchises and Venus. On the morning of the battle of Pharsalia, Caesar made a vow to build a temple to his goddess ancestor. Pompey was defeated completely and Caesar built the new Forum (Between the old one and the Quirinal), in the centre of which rose the Temple to Venus Genetrix. For centuries this temple remained a splendid monument, worthy of the fame and magnificence of the first Caesar. Among the numerous works of art placed in it, was the statue of Venus Genetrix, by Archesilaus, one of the most celebrated Greek sculptors, and one of Cleopatra. The temple was rebuilt by Trajan and inaugurated with the Trajan column on the 12th of May of the year 113. The excavations of the past years have revealed traces of the Forum and of the Temple of Venus Genetrix. For the occasion, the **statue of Julius Caesar,** copied in bronze from the one in the Capitol, was placed on a pedestal in the excavated ruins of the Forum. The Perpetual Dictator towers here in the glory of Rome. After almost 2000 years Caesar is still a popular hero.

The **Basilica Argentaria,** added by Trajan to the Temple of Venus Genetrix, was the residence and meeting place for bankers and money-changers. « Argentarii » was the name given to public and private bankers in ancient Rome.

The **FORUM OF AUGUSTUS.** After the assassination of Caesar, the chief of the conspirators, Cassius, went to Syria and Brutus to Macedonia to take possession of the two provinces. In 42 B.C. their armies met those of Mark Anthony and Octavian at Philippi: and as Caesar had done at Pharsalia, Augustus did at Philippi: he made a vow to Mars, Father of the Roman people. Caesar's murderers met their fate, Brutus fell on his own sword and Cassius ordered his freed-slave to kill him. Augustus kept his vow and built the Temple to Mars Ultor, which became the centre of a new Forum. It was dedicated on the first of August, his month, in the year 2 B.C. The most recent excavations have brought to light imposing traces of this Forum and its gigantic temple that Ovid described for us. Augustus was the first Emperor (30 B.C. to 14 A.D.). During his reign, Jesus Christ was born.

In the **FORUM OF NERVA** (96-98) a part of its surrounding wall, known as the « Colonnacce » because of the protruding columns that decorate it, has been restored. They formed part of the Temple of Minerva, whose destruction was ordered by Paul V to get the necessary marble to build the fountain on the Janiculum. During recent excavations, a large area was exposed giving interesting topographical information and showing a well preserved part of the « Cloaca Massima ».

We are now in front of one of the greatest wonders of Roman times: the **COLOSSEUM.** This immense amphitheatre, of which we still admire the ancient splendour, was begun by Vespasian in A.D. 72 and finished by his son Titus in A.D. 80. Hebrew prisoners were employed in its construction. Its real name is **Flavian Amphitheatre,** commonly called Colosseum perhaps because the Colossus of Nero was in its vicinity. There is scarcely a page of Roman history that is not connected with the Colosseum, which became the symbol of the city and its life. Thus in the 8th century the Venerable Bede said: « While stands the Colosseum, Rome shall stand; when falls the Colosseum, Rome shall fall; and when Rome falls, with it shall fall the World ». After the sacking of the Normans (1084), nothing but a

TRAJAN'S FORUM was erected by the Emperor to celebrate his victory over the Dacians. This grandiose construction is the work of the architect Apollodorus of Damascus.

THE COLOSSEUM - Past and present.

Inside of the Colosseum - **THE SUBTERRANEAN.** ►

skeleton remained of antique classic Rome; the Colosseum was abandoned and for years it was used as a quarry for building material. Benedict XIV (1740-1758), in order to save what was left, consecrated the old amphitheatre as a « Via Crucis », raising a cross in the centre of the ground that history has consecrated to the names of innumerable martyrs, who gave their lives for their faith before thousands of blood-thirsty spectators. The « Ludi Circenses » were the favorite shows of the Romans, games that were probably invented in the last days of the Republic, with the intention of developing the war-like spirit that had made them the conquerors of the world. This was the origin of the professional gladiators, who were trained to fight to the death, while wild beasts of every sort increased the horror of the show. Dion Cassius says that 9000 wild animals were killed during the hundred days of festivity to celebrate the dedication of this building. After the animals were killed, and removed, the arena was often filled with water in order to stage naval battles. The great Emperor Con-

A view of the inside of the Amphitheatre during the famous "LUDI CIRCENSES" (Circus Games).

stantine and his successors tried to stop the gladiatorial fights, but at first the Romans would not give up their customary shows. At the beginning of the 5th century, a monk named Telemachus, who had come from the East, entered the arena one day and tried to place himself between the gladiators. He turned to the people, begging them to stop these horrible shows. There were sarcastic protests and insults; the intruder, a great martyr to the cause of humanity, was stoned to death. But from that day, these shows ended.

The Colosseum, of elliptical form, is 205 yards in its longest diameter and 170 yards in its shortest. On the outside there were three rows of arches, respectively adorned with Doric, Ionic and Corinthian columns, and a fourth floor was adorned with Corinthian pilasters. An ellipse of 80 arches formed the outer circuit. Four arches corresponding to the four semi-diameters, led to a large corridor that went all around it. In the centre of one side of the podium called « suggestum », was the Emperor's seat; the rest of the podium was

The INSIDE OF THE COLOSSEUM as it is today.

An **AERIAL VIEW OF THE COLOSSEUM.** Note the extent of its surface when compared to the surrounding houses.

occupied by senators and patricians. Then there were the places for cavaliers, civil and military tribunes. There were also special places for married people, for young men accompanied by their tutors, for families and servants, for women and for the plebeians. The Colosseum was normally uncovered; but in the case of rain or during dog-days it was protected by an immense velarium, which was fixed by two squads of sailors belonging to the fleets of Ravenna and Cape Misenum. These two squads resided permanently in Rome in order to participate in the naval fights.

When the amphitheatre was at the climax of its glory, it must have been a stupendous sight of Roman splendour. But even to-day, after so many centuries, the Colosseum is the pride of Rome and the marvel of visitors.

The name, **ROMAN FORUM,** designated the group of monuments (almost all of the Republican era) whose ruins are between the Capitol, the Imperial Forums, the Colosseum and the Palatine. The Forum was crossed by the **Via Sacra** which led to the Capitoline hill.

◄ **Inside of the Colosseum - THE SUBTERRANEAN.**

These stones are witnesses of all the tempests of the human spirit. These ruins show us how Empires rose and fell and how Rome was present in the greatest epochs of the world, epochs of art, history, religion and humanity.

The **Arch of Constantine** was erected by the Senate and the Roman people at the extreme limit of the Forum on the Via Sacra, in memory of the victory of Costantine at Ponte Milvio in 312. Almost all the marble was taken from the arches of Trajan and Marcus Aurelius and other monuments, so that the Arch of Constantine was derisively called Aesop's Jay. The most interesting part of this splendid monument and the best preserved, is the inscription: « To the Emperor Caesar Flavius Constantine Maximus, "pius, felix, augustus", the Senate and the people of Rome dedicate this notable arch in honour of his triumphs, because, by Divine inspiration and greatness of mind, he freed the Republic by just wars from tyranny and from factions ». Now the magistrates of the city were pagans and they knew that Constantine, if not a Christian, favoured Christianity. They did not want to name Christ on a public monument and yet they did not want to offend the Emperor by naming pagan gods. So they found a way to satisfy both sides by saying « Divine inspiration ».

Near the Arch of Constantine there is a circle on the paving. There was a fountain there called « Meta Sudans » which existed in Nero's time and was rebuilt by Domitian. The gladiators washed themselves at this fountain. Further on, at the end of the street of the Imperial Forums, a block of travertine on the paving shows where the « Colossus of Nero » stood, brought there by Hadrian. This famous statue was erected by Nero in the atrium of his « Domus Aurea » (Golden House).

The finest religious building in Rome was the twin **Temple of Venus and Roma** of which the ruins still remain. The columns, scattered on the ground, and now reconstructed and erected on the same spot, give us the idea of the portico that surrounded the temple. It was designed by Hadrian, who had the Colossus of Nero removed to obtain the necessary space. It is said that the Emperor showed his design to Apollodorus, who created Trajan's Forum.

The great architect pointed out that if the seated statues should stand up, they would hit their heads on the ceiling.

On the ruins of the Temple of Roma, was built, in the VII century, the church of « Santa Maria Nova », dedicated at the beginning of the XVIII century to **Santa Francesca Romana**. The « Antiquarium Forense » is in the adjacent convent.

The **Arch of Titus,** that the Senate erected after his death, recalls the conquest of Jerusalem. In the interior are two fine bas-reliefs: the Emperor on his triumphal chariot and the procession of Jewish prisoners carrying the famous candelabrum with seven branches.

The immense **Basilica of Maxentius,** also called of Constantine, is the last edifice bearing the impression of the magnificence of ancient Rome. It was begun by Maxentius and finished after the victory by Constantine. This superb construction of the 4th century is said to have given Bramante his inspiration for St. Peter's. It is mainly characterized by its powerful, wide vaults.

The **Temple of Antoninus and Faustina** is the best preserved in the Forum. The loss of Faustina embittered the Emperor, who often used to say he would have preferred to live in a desert with her than in a palace without her. After her death, the Emperor deified her and erected this magnificent temple in her honour. This temple was later changed into the church of **San Lorenzo in Miranda.**

Many pagan temples were changed into Christian churches. The old church of **SS. Cosma and Damiano** was established by Felix IV in

An interplay of light and shadow created by the Colosseum's succession of arches. Further back can be seen the ruins of the TEMPLE OF VENUS AND ROMA.

THE ROMAN FORUM, centre of the city's public life in ancient times.

527 in the Templum Sacrae Urbis that Emperor Vespasian had erected in the Forum Pacis or Forum of Vespasian. The vestibule rises over the round **temple of Romulus** and still has the bronze door with the original lock. The **Sepulcretum** or Archaic Necropolis dates from the 9th century B.C.

The **Temple of Vesta,** circular in form, was built, according to tradition, by Numa, who placed there the Palladium (image of Minerva) and other sacred objects brought to Italy by Aeneas. The safety of the city depended on their safe keeping. The Vestals had to keep the fire burning. They were six, chosen from patrician maidens, daughters of free parents. They enjoyed special privileges, but if one broke the vow of chastity, she was buried alive in the Field of Villains. Near the temple are the ruins of the **House of the Vestal Virgins** and we can still see many statues and inscrip-

26

tions. In one of these, the name of the Vestal has been erased, leaving only the first letter C. The prince of Christian poets, Prudentius, recalls in his poems the Vestal Claudia who became a Christian and who was considered an honour and a glory to the faithful in Rome. He describes the scene of her visit to the basilica of the martyr, St. Lawrence. It is possible that this Claudia may be the same to whom a statue was raised in 364 in « homage to her chastity and profound knowledge of religion, etc. ». The name was erased perhaps because she was converted to Christianity. The **Temple of Julius Caesar,** that Octavianus erected in memory of his uncle, was begun in B.C. 42 on the spot where the Dictator's body was burned, and consecrated in B. C. 29 at the same time as the Arch of Augustus.

The **Regia,** according to tradition, was the house of Numa Pompilius and, later the residence

THE ARCH OF CONSTANTINE, erected by the Roman Senate to commemorate Constantine's victory over Maxentius (313 A.D.).

FORUM

1. Curia
2. Arch of Septimius Severus
3. The Rostra
4. Temple of Vespasian
5. Via Sacra

6. Temple of Saturnus
7. Column of Phocas
8. Basilica Julia
9. Basilica Aemilia
10. Temple of Julius Caesar

11. Temple of Vesta

MANUM

12. Temple of Castor and Pollux
13. S. Maria Antiqua
14. Temple of Augustus
15. Temple of Antoninus and Faustina
16. Temple of Romulus

17. Temple of Venus and Roma
18. House of the Vestal Virgins
19. Basilica of Maxentius
20. Colosseum
21. Arch of Titus

22. Palatinum

THE ROMAN FORUM. The white remains of temples and marble palaces recall the ancient splendour of the city.

The Roman Forum. THE ARCH OF SEPTIMIUS SEVERUS was erected in honour of Septimius and his ►
sons, Caracalla and Geta.

of the "Pontifex Maximus". On the walls are the "fasti consolari" in sculpture. The inscription is in archaic Latin.

The **Temple of Castor and Pollux,** also called the Temple of the Twins, was erected in B. C. 484 to celebrate the victory of Aulus Postumius over the Latins, in the battle at Lake Regillus. The three columns and part of the cornice, very fine work in Pentelic marble, are of the time of Trajan or Hadrian. — It is related that two young men on two white horses appeared during the battle: they were the twins, Castor and Pollux. They rode to Rome, quenched the thirst of their horses at the **fountain of Juturna,** announcing to the Romans the victory of their arms, and then disappeared.

St. Maria Antiqua is one of the oldest Roman basilicas built by transforming an imperial edifice annexed to the Atrium Minervae in the 5th century. The church consists of an atrium,

The Roman Forum. The three columns on the left are the remains of the TEMPLE OF CASTOR AND POLLUX, those on the right belonged to the TEMPLE OF SATURN.

Near the ARCH OF TITUS: Shining columns stretch ▶ towards the sky like the strings of a harp.

a narthex, three naves and a presbytery. On the walls of the apse, we note the frescoes of the 8th century, greatly deteriorated. The church was buried by a landslide in the 9th century and was only brought to light by the excavations of 1900. — To the right of St. Maria Antiqua are the ruins of the **temple of Augustus.**

The **Basilica Julia.** In a conflict between Milo and Clodius on the Appian way, Clodius was killed and his body brought to Rome. There was a popular uprising and part of the Forum was set on fire. Thus Caesar found the space for his new constructions. The Basilica Julia was erected in 46 B. C. and finished by Augustus. After all the vicissitudes of the Forum, the vast basilica was restored in A. D. 277.

The **Comitium,** the place where the representatives of the people gathered for public discussions, was also at first the tribunal of Rome. It was here, in the first days of the Republic, that Junius Brutus condemned to death his two sons, who had been denounced for plotting the return of King Tarquinius. Here the beautiful Virginia was stabbed by her father. In this square, the most powerful voices of Rome resounded; Cicero, prince of orators, made his famous speeches of the second and third Catilinaria. Here the head of the great writer and politician was exposed to public view after his assassination. There are many memories here of legendary Roman history. There is more history in this place than in entire kingdoms. It may be called the Olympus of the History of Rome.

The **Rostra,** of which the large platform is still visible, were erected by Caesar in 44 B. C. just before his death. The tribunes from which orators, political men and leaders addressed the crowds were called Rostra. In the Republican era, the tribunes were of wood and were situated in the Comitium. In 338 B. C. it as decorated with the prows of Latin ships captured at the battle of Antium. « Ad rostra! » became the cry of the Roman people to call a meeting.

In 1899 there was discovered the famous **Lapis Niger** which marked the supposed burial place of Romulus. It is a sepulchral monument of the time of the Kings, on which is engraved the most ancient Latin epigraph we have.

The **Column of Phocas** is the last classical memory of the Forum. At the beginning of the 7th century the Byzantine Emperor Phocas had allowed the Pope Boniface IV, to change the Pantheon into a Christian church. The Romans, in token of gratitude, took a beautiful column from the portico of some old building and erected it to the tyrant Phocas, who ended his days on the scaffold at Byzantium.

The **Arch of Septimius Severus,** complicated and over-ornate, shows the advancing decadence in Roman art. It was erected in honour of Septimius and his two sons, Caracalla and Geta. In the inscription is the record of an imperial tragedy: after Geta was killed, Caracalla had his name removed. Septimius Severus reigned 18 years (193-211) and died a natural death, a rare thing in the 3rd century. He had brilliant military successes everywhere. He was born at Leptis Magna in Africa and died in York (Eboracum), England.

The **Miliarium Aureum** is the column on which the distances to the principal cities of the Empire were cut, in gold letters.

The **Temple of Saturn** was erected by the Consul Titus Larcius on the 17th of December 498 B. C. It was always used as the Public Treasury. The ensigns of the Legions and decrees of the Senate were also kept here. In an underground cell were kept the sacred treasures, among which was the gold for ransom given to Brennus and retaken by the valour of Camillus. A tremendous curse would strike the sacrilegious hand that tried to carry it off for any reason, save to repel a new Gallic invasion. Caesar easily obtained

The Roman Forum. The three columns of the TEMPLE OF THE DIOSCURI are still reflected in the great pool of the HOUSE OF THE VESTAL VIRGINS, girl priestesses who in far-distant times guarded the sacred fire of Rome.

The Roman Forum is crossed by the SACRED WAY which led up to the Capitol

the consent of the Senate and wanted to appropriate the treasure, but he found the tribune Metellus inflexibly barring the way, protesting that no one should pass except over his dead body. « The Gauls have been conquered once for all » cried Caesar, and had the door beaten down with axes. Metellus, knowing that the dictator's blows were more rapid than his words, prudently withdrew. In 42 B. C. the Temple was rebuilt on a larger scale. We see it today as it was reconstructed in the 4th century by the Christians and used as a Public Treasury.

The **Temple of Vespasian** was erected by his son, Domitian, in 94 and restored by Septimius Severus. Only three columns remain.

The **Temple of Concord** was erected by Furius Camillus, the conqueror of the Gauls in 367 B. C. to commemorate the pact concluded at Monte Sacro between plebeians and patricians. In this temple the Senate met to hear Cicero's last speech against Catiline.

The **Tullian** or **Mamertine Prisons** go back to ancient times. It was thought that they were called « Tullian » from the Roman king, Servius Tullius; instead the name derives from « tullus » meaning a vein of water. The cell that held the vein of water was made into a very secure State prison, by means of construction over it and next to it. The entrance to these horrible cells was formed by two holes in the ceiling through which the pri-

The Roman Forum. Ruins and columns ►
of the **TEMPLE OF THE DIOSCURI**.

soners were thrown down; the stairs are medieval.

Near by, the **Church of SS. Martina and Luca,** since the 7th century, occupies the place of the former « Secretarium Senatus ». The superior church was reconstructed in the 17th century.

The **Curia** that Pope Honorius I had changed into a Christian church, was founded by Tullus Hostilius (Curia Hostilia), reconstructed by Sulla, by Julius Caesar and finally by Diocletian.

The statue of the Goddess Victory, brought from Taranto, was placed here by Augustus and was still here at the time of Gratianus (375-383) who removed it, to the great indignation of the pagans, who considered it the palladium of their faith. Q. Aurelius Symmachus, the last champion of paganism, sent a strong protest to Valentinianus II (375-392), demanding that the statue be put back in its place. St. Ambrose wrote to the Emperor that the adorers of false gods were already forgotten by their gods.

In 1931, all the parts that had been added to transform it into a church were removed and great care was taken to restore this interesting historical building to its original form.

The **Basilica Aemilia** was founded in 179 B.C. by Emilius Lepidus and Fulvius Nobilior. Rebuilt and restored several times, especially by the Aemilia family, it was destroyed definitely by fire in the beginning of the 5th century. It was one of the most splendid buildings of the Forum. In front of the Basilica is a small round pedestal of the shrine of Venus Cloacina on the spot where the Cloaca Maxima entered the Forum.

After the fall of the Roman Empire, the Forum did not lose its importance, notwithstanding barbarian devastations. St. Fulgentius of Ruspe was in the Forum in the year 500, at the moment when Theodoric, King of Italy, seated on a splendid throne, received the homage of the Senate. The sight of such grandeur and magnificence so impressed the Saint that he exclaimed: « If terrestrial Rome shines in such majesty of monuments, oh, how beautiful must celestial Jerusalem be! » Theodoric, in fact, did not like to be considered a barbarian and kept alive the admiration of Roman spirit. Again, in 608, while Italy was under the domination of the Longobards, the column to Emperor Phocas was raised in the Forum. It was then, in the succeeding centuries, that the decline of the Forum accelerated, one of the causes being the terrible earthquake of 851 at the time of Pope Leo IV. Nor were the Romans of the tenth century in such spiritual, political or economic circumstances as to worry over the condition of the Forum. In 1084 the Normans, called by Gregory VII who was besieged by Henry IV (of Italy) laid the city to waste, sacking and burning with devastating fury. Some years later, a French writer said: « Rome exists no longer; some of it still stands, some has fallen but what remains cannot be restored and what is fallen cannot be rebuilt ». It was the end of the Forum!

The **PALATINE** was the centre of Rome in two distinct eras: that of the Kings and that of the Emperors. During the Republic, the Patrician families dwelt on the Palatine. Quintus Hortensius, the celebrated orator who emulated Cicero, lived here in a house given him by Augustus. When Augustus became Emperor, he made his imperial residence on the Palatine. Afterwards Tiberius, Caligula, the Flavii and Septimius Severus built palaces here.

The Palatine was the cradle of Rome. Here, according to legend, Romulus traced with a plough the square outline of the first city; here was the seat of the Kings. Because of this the hill was chosen as the residence of the Caesars and up to Septimius Severus, no Emperor left it. Only Nero built his Domus Aurea elsewhere but it was never finished nor inhabited by him.

38

The immense brickwork vaults of the BASILICA OF MAXENTIUS, provide glimpses of the sky and the ► CHURCH OF S. FRANCESCA ROMANA.

Today, this cradle of Rome, through modern excavations, is coming to light again and even its ruins speak eloquently to the visitor's memory.

At the foot of the hill, we see the elliptical form of the **CIRCUS MAXIMUS,** where the horse races took place. It was built under the kings, and more and more enlarged during the Republic and the Empire: under the reign of Constantine, it could contain more than 100.000 spectators.

The **FABRICIUS BRIDGE,** constructed in 62 B.C., is Rome's most ancient bridge. It joins the Tiberina Island to the banks of the Tiber, here known as Lungotevere Cenci.

second itinerary

THEATRE OF MARCELLUS
ISLAND IN THE TIBER
ST. PAUL'S
E.U.R.

On the left side, at the beginning of via del Teatro di Marcello, a rock rises which is thought to be the famous « Rupe Tarpea », whence the traitress Tarpea was precipitated (8th century B.C.) as since all the other traitors of Rome.

At the side of the Theatre of Marcellus, we find the ruins of the **Portico of Octavia,** mother of Marcellus, erected by her brother Augustus. The propylaeum of the portico serves as atrium to the church of **Sant'Angelo in Pescheria** (name derived from the fish market in front of it), founded in the 8th century.

The **Theatre of Marcellus** is the only antique theatre left in Rome. It is a fine edifice, erected by Augustus and dedicated to his sister Octavia's son, Marcellus, who died at the age of twenty two greatly mourned and immortalized by Virgil's poem. Later on, this theatre served as a model for the construction of the Colosseum. We can still admire a part of the exterior curved wall with its double row of Doric and Ionic arches, surmounted on the upper part by the Savelli castle (later of the Orsini), erected by Baldassarre Peruzzi.

We come to the Tiber and see the characteristic **ISOLA TIBERINA** (Island in the Tiber). On the famous temple of Esculapius, the Greek god of medicine, once the centre for pilgrimages of sick persons, rises the church of **St. Bartholomew on the Island.**

The **Ponte Fabricio** (Quattro Capi) erected in 62 B.C. still almost intact today, and **Ponte Cestio** (46 B.C.) unite the island to the city. The place occupied today by the Palatine Bridge was formerly the site of the **Ponte Sublicio,** noted for the legend of Horace Cocles.

On the other side we see the **Synagogue,** built in 1904 in Assyro-Babylonian style, with its grey cupola of aluminium.

Behind it is the **Ghetto,** the part of the city where the Jews were segregated for several centuries and where the lower class Jews still live.

Let us return to via del Teatro Marcello and visit the **FORUM BOARIUM** (cattle market). The **House of Crescentii** built in the 10th century by the powerful Crescenzi family, is an interesting piece of medieval construction, perhaps a fort guarding the river. Its decorations are formed by antique fragments from several Roman buildings.

The temple called **Fortuna Virile** was not dedicated to this divinity but rather to Mater Matuta. It dates from the Ist century B.C. and is a fine example of the Greek-Italian architecture of Republican times. In A.D. 872, a certain Stephen made it into a Christian church, dedicated to St. Maria Egiziaca. It was then given to the Armenians.

The church of **St. George,** called in **Velabro,** because there was a marsh here of that name, suffered from time and neglect but has recently been restored. It dates from the 7th

41

The ancient Sublicius Bridge, near TIBERINA ISLAND, where the Emperor Otto III. (10th century A.D.) erected the Church of St. Bartholomew on the ruins of the Temple of Aesculapius

century. The fine bell-tower and Ionic portico are of the 12th century.

The **Arch of the Argentari,** a curious monument covered with poor reliefs, was erected by the money-changers and shop-keepers of the Forum Boarium to Septimius Severus and Julia Domna, whose portraits are seen on the reliefs. Opposite is the access to the **Cloaca Massima. Janus Quadrifrons,** an arched passage with four façades, was built in the time of Constantine.

St. Mary's in Cosmedin, one of the gems of Medieval Rome, rises on the ruins of a temple, perhaps the temple of Ceres. The picturesque austere interior gives us a clear idea of a primitive church (8th century). The **bell-tower** in Romanesque style, of the 12th century, is one of the loveliest of its kind in Rome.

At the left of the portico is a marble mask called **Bocca della Verità** (mouth of truth); according to popular belief it was said that any one putting his hand in this mouth and swearing falsely, could not withdraw it.

In front of the church is the beautiful round temple that tradition dedicated to **Vesta,** perhaps for its resemblance to the one in the

The MOUTH OF TRUTH. This marble mask, of which popular tradition preserves an amusing legend, is to be found in the Church of S. Maria in Cosmedin.

Forum, but there is nothing to prove it.

The **Pyramid** of Caius Cestius, at the Porta Ostiense, that in medieval times was known as the tomb of Romulus, was erected in the last years of the Republic as a tomb for Caius Cestius Praetor. Tribune of the people and member of the College of the Septemviri Epulones, according to the two inscriptions.

ST. PAUL'S (San Paolo fuori le Mura or **Basilica Ostiense)** is one of the most illustrious churches in Rome, erected where the great Apostle was buried. Emperor Constantine first built a church over the tomb of St. Paul. A larger basilica was erected at the end of the 4th century. In the inscription on the mosaic of the triumphal arch, we read that Theodosius began it. Honorius finished it and under Leo I (440-461). Placidia restored and decorated it: This splendid basilica, one of the wonders of the world, was destroyed by fire in 1823. It was rebuilt on the same foundations and to the same design.

The large **quadriporticus** composed of 150 columns, with the statue of St. Paul in the centre at once gives the impression of the typical Roman basilica.

The mosaic **façade** is a glitter of gold, colour and light. In the narthex, the bronze-door is by Emilio Maraini (1930).

The **interior of the basilica,** consisting of one

The stupendous view of the INSIDE OF THE BASILICA OF ST. PAUL.

THE BASILICA OF ST. PAUL OUTSIDE THE WALLS. The richly decorated arches of the quadruple portico and the golden mosaic blend particularly well with the severe statue of St. Paul.

BASILICA OF ST. PAUL.   The CLOISTER by Vassalletto.

nave and four aisles, is sumptuous and impressive: the eye is enchanted by the endless rows of columns, the mystic light from the double row of alabaster windows above them, the magnificent white and gold ceiling in Renaissance style, the shining marble pavement, reflecting the light and under the chancel arch the delightful canopy against the background of the gold mosaics of the apse. Between the windows and the columns, a row of mosaic medallions portray the long series of Popes from St. Peter to John XXIII.

Inside the façade, there are four columns of alabaster sustaining the immense canopy by Poletti that covered the present one, and two columns sustaining the cornice. They are exceedingly precious.

The mosaics of the **chancel arch** date from the 5th century. They were executed by order of the Empress Galla Placidia. After they were damaged by fire in 1823, accurately taken down and not too well restored. Later they were put up again and now form one of the glories of the basilica.

The **canopy,** in Gothic style, raised on four columns of porphyry, admirable in harmony of line, is the unsurpassable work of Arnolfo di Cambio (13th century).

The **Cosmatesque cloister,** by Vassalletto, restored in 1907, revealing the ancient roof, must be considered one of the most noteworthy works of Roman marble sculptors, a real masterpiece for the elegant moulding, the richness and the elegance of its mosaics and its carvings.

The **façade** on via Ostiense, and the bell-tower, are by Luigi Poletti (1850).

Following the « Via del Mare » towards Ostia, we cross after some kilometres the most modern monumental residence quarter of Rome, called **E.U.R.** (Esposizione Universale di Roma). Imposing buildings, perfect sport installations, among which the splendid **Sports Palace,** and an artificial lake, are the pride of this new Rome.

EUR. PALAZZO DELLA CIVILTA' E DEL LAVORO. This modern building, on account of its form and its 216 arches, is often referred to as the "square Colosseum".

A typical Roman carriage, locally known as "botticella", near the PINCINE GATE at the top end of Via Veneto. Villa Borghese, Rome's most magnificent park, can be seen behind the gate

third itinerary

QUIRINAL
VIA VENETO
TERMINI STATION
ST. MARY MAJOR

The **QUIRINAL** is so called from Quirinus, the Sabine name of the God Mars who was from remote ages venerated on this hill, where, under Titus Tatius, the Sabines had emigrated. At the end of the Republic, Quirinus became identified with Romulus, son of Mars.

The immense **Quirinal Palace,** begun by Gregory XIII in 1547, was the Summer residence of the Popes until 1870. Then it became the residence of the King. Now the President of the Republic lives there.

Here we admire the works by Maderno, Bernini, Guido Reni, Giulio Romano etc. On the square the beautiful **Fountain with the obelisk** and the statues of the Dioscuri, Castor and Pollux.

On the right, the elegant and majestic **Palace of the Consulta,** by Fuga.

Descending the steep via Quattro Fontane we find on the right the **BARBERINI PALACE** begun under Urban VIII to a design by Maderno and continued by Borromini and Bernini untll 1640.

It is now the seat of the National Gallery of Rome. Among the many paintings exhibited, ranging from the 12th to the 16th centuries, there are some which have acquired world fame, such as *Fornarina by Raphael, **Christ and the Adulteress** by Tintoretto, a **Madonna with the Holy Child** by Simone Martini, Fra Angelico's triptych with the **Ascension, Pentecost,** and the **Last Judgment.** In the hall of

the Palace one should not fail to look at the beautiful fresco painted on the ceiling by Pietro da Cortona and representing the **Triumph of Divine Providence** (1640).

At the end of the slope we reach the **Piazza Barberini** with the very original **Fountain of the Triton** by Bernini.

We cross it diagonally to reach the aristocratic **VIA VENETO.** At the beginning, on the right, is the **fountain of the Bees,** by Bernini and then the **Capuchin Church** with St. Michael by Guido Reni and the Ecstasy of St. Francis, by Domenichino. Underneath the church, is the **Cemetery of the Capuchins.**

The majestic ruins of the **Baths of Diocletian,** that in antiquity surpassed in extent and splendour all the others in Rome, remain to testify to their original grandeur and magnificence. These baths were erected in 303.

One of the large rooms of these baths was transformed by Michelangelo into the church of **ST. MARY OF THE ANGELS** (1563-66).

The modern **ESEDRA** which is to-day called « Piazza della Repubblica », occupies the place of the old Esedra. In the centre is the large **Fountain of the Naiads** by Rutelli, made in 1911, one of the latest fountains that are the joys of Rome.

At the end of the nearby « piazza dei Cinquecento » rises the very modern façade of the **Stazione Termini.**

As we go down the via Nazionale, we turn to

VIA VITTORIO VENETO is famous throughout the world for its elegance; it is also regarded as the drawing room of Roman and international high society. Its coffee houses and hotels are among the most elegant to be found in the city.

the left into the via Agostino Depretis and come to the **Viminal Palace,** now the Ministry of Home Affairs. To the left, on via Viminale is the **Opera House,** the first of Rome and one of the best in Italy. Following the via Agostino Depretis we admire the **Apse of Santa Maria Maggiore.**

SANTA MARIA MAGGIORE, the fourth church of Rome, is so called because it is the largest dedicated to the Virgin. It is the only Roman church that has kept its original form and character, notwithstanding some decorations added later.

In the night of August 5th, 352, the Virgin appeared in a dream to the patrician John and to Pope Liberius (352-366) commanding them to build a church on the spot where on the following day snow would fall. The miracle took place and the basilica was erected. This poetic legend is of late date and was recorded in the medieval mosaics that, much restored, may still be admired in the loggia of the vestibule.

The basilica, also called « Liberiana », dates from the time of Sixtus III (432-440).

The **façade,** by Fuga, is pleasing. It has a

The elegant FOUNTAIN OF THE NAIADS in Republic Square. The white marble of the facade of the Termini Station can be seen in the background.

One of the four splendid nymphs of the Fountain of the Naiads.

porch with five portals, divided by pillars, adorned by columns and with a loggia above it, with three large arcades. Towering above it is the tallest belfry in Rome, built in Romanesque style. The **interior,** formed by a nave and two aisles, is a magnificent sight. At the end of a double row of columns, under the chancel arch, is the great **canopy** by Fuga, sustained by four precious columns of porphyry. The **ceiling,** by Julian Sangallo, was gilded with the first gold brought from America. Along the architrave a series of thirty-six mosaics, reproducing scenes of the Old Testament is connected with those of the **chancel arch** that reproduce scenes of the New Testament. All these mosaics are of the 5th century and are of exceptional importance and

beauty. The pavement of the basilica is very fine cosmatesque work.

The **Confessional** in front of the high altar was decorated in 1874 by Vespignani, who used the richest and rarest marbles. Behind the metal grill are the celebrated relics of the Crib, consisting of five pieces of the Manger in which the Christ-child was placed at his birth, enclosed in a silver urn designed by Valadier. Opposite is the large kneeling **Statue of Pius IX,** by Jacometti.

The **High altar** under the great canopy is the sarcophagus containing the bones of St. Mark, the Evangelist. In the apse with ogival windows we admire the **Triumph of Mary,** a fine mosaic by I. Turriti (1295).

◄ **THE FOUNTAIN OF THE TRITON, in** Piazza Barberini.   **THE TERMINI STATION.**

The **BASILICA OF S. MARIA MAGGIORE** is the only church to have kept intact its form of an early Christian church. The facade is the work of Fuga. The Basilica was erected by Pope Sixtus III. (432-440) in honour of the Virgin Mary.

ST. PETER IN CHAINS
COLLE OPPIO
ST. CLEMENT
ST. JOHN IN LATERANUM

The basilica of **ST. PIETRO IN VINCOLI** (St. Peter in chains) was due to the generosity of an Imperial matron, Eudoxia, daughter of Theodosius the Young, and wife of Valentinian III. Her mother had sent her the chains used by Herod to chain Peter which she had received from Juvenal, bishop of Jerusalem. To preserve these chains, young Eudoxia erected this basilica, then called « Eudoxiana », but to-day commonly known as « St. Peter in Chains ».

The nave is divided by twenty columns taken from an old monument.

To the left of the entrance is the **Tomb of Anthony Pollaiolo** (1432-1498), sculptor, jeweller, painter, engraver, who settled in Rome in 1489, where he did many works, among which the large monument to Sixtus IV that is now in the new Museum Petriano. His brother who helped him, is also buried here.

Every one comes to this church to see the celebrated * **Statue of Moses,** with which the gigantic genius of Michelangelo brought Renaissance sculpture to the apex of magnificence. This austere chief of his own people, this just legislator who was accustomed to speak with God, is seated here, still radiant with the sight of God, with such an air of biblical majesty, that nobody can help being dominated in his senses and penetrated to the very depths of his soul.

In 1505 the artist was called to Rome by Julius II who wanted him to make a Mausoleum for himself worthy of ancient Rome: but he suddenly changed his mind. He thought that a new St. Peter's would be better than a Mausoleum, to perpetuate his glory.

The monument as we see it now, was erected by the Duke of Urbino, nephew of Julius II. What remains of the glorious plans of the great artist? Only the shade of a sublime project! The two statues of « Rachel and Leah », symbols of active and contemplative life, were designed by Michelangelo; all the rest was done by his pupils.

On the **COLLE OPPIO** is the access to the celebrated « Domus Aurea » of Nero, an imposing, fantastic group of buildings that extended from the Palatine to the Esquiline. The central palace built here was destroyed in 104 by a great fire. Over it were built the foundations for the construction of the **Baths of Trajan,** of which only a few ruins remain.

The **BASILICA OF ST. CLEMENT,** mentioned by St. Jerome in the 4th century, is one of the most interesting in Rome from an artistic and archeological point of view. It was almost buried under the enormous quantity of debris accumulated in that zone after the terrible fire caused by the Normans in 1084, but was rebuilt in the 12th century by Paschal II on a higher level. The new basilica was built in

The Tomb of Pope Julius II., the work of Michelangelo. The Pope, a member of the della Rovere family, commissioned the tomb during his lifetime. The centrepiece of the tomb is constituted by the powerful and majestic figure of MOSES, leader of the Jewish people.

the original form with all the architectural elements it was possible to save, so that it remains, in spite of restorations and modification of more recent date, a rare example of a typical early Christian basilica.

There are notable works of art of the Renaissance in this basilica. In the first chapel of the left aisle, we admire the famous frescoes of Masolino da Panicale (1431), formery attributed to Masaccio. In the centre to the left, St. Christopher; on the central wall, a dramatic Crucifixion; on the later walls, to the right, episodes from the life of St. Ambrose, and St. Catherine, to the left. On the altar a Madonna, by Sassoferrato. In the chapel at the end of the nave, the Madonna of the Rosary by Sebastian Conca. Further on in front of the last arch, the Tomb of Cardinal Venerio whose columns belonged to the original canopy. In the right aisle, besides the Tomb of Archbishop Brusati, by L. Capponi (1485) is the Monument to Cardinal Roverella, his uncle, a fine work by A. Bregno and G. Dalmata.

Here we are in the piazza di S. Giovanni in Laterano.

The **LATERAN** was the residence of the Popes

The famous CHAINS with which St. Peter was imprisoned during the reign of Herod are conserved in this bronze urn.

The so-called "FONTANA DELLA NAVICELLA", a fountain reproducing an ancient Roman ship. Behind it can be seen the entrance to the Church of S. Maria in Domnica.

up to 1305 i.e. until they moved from Rome to Avignon. Their palace, the « Patriarchium », was pulled down in 1596 by Domenico Fontana by command of Pope Sixtus V, who ordered the present one to be built.

The **Lateran obelisk** is the tallest of the thirteen that stand in as many squares of Rome. It was erected in 1449 B. C. by Tutmes III and his son Tutmes IV of the XVIII dynasty at Thebes in Egypt. Sixtus V had it erected here by Fontana.

On the right of the square is the **Baptistery.**

It was erected by the Emperor Constantine where, according to an erroneous tradition, he had been christened by Saint Silvester. Later on, it was rebuilt by order of Sixtus III (432-440) and afterwards several popes had it restored. It is an octagonal structure. Eight columns of porphyry sustain the cornice and another eight of marble the dome.

To the left of the square is the **Scala Santa.** According to tradition it is the same flight of marble steps which Jesus ascended in the house of Pilate; it was brought to Rome by the pious Empress Helena. The twenty-eight steps may only be ascended kneeling. At the top of the stairs is the private chapel of the Popes which formed a part of old Patriarchium, called the « Sancta Sanctorum », richly decorated by the Cosmati in 1278. At the sides of staircase are two splendid groups by Jacometti: the « Kiss of Judas », and « Pilate showing Christ to the People ».

ST. JOHN IN THE LATERAN is the Cathedral of Rome, the mother of all churches in Rome and in the world. Founded by Constantine and called the « Basilica of the Saviour » during the time of Silvester (314-335) it has been destroyed and rebuilt many times. The actual basilica dates from the 17th century.

The imposing façade in travertine was constructed in 1735 by Alexander Galilei, who used all his architectural ability on the portico. At the left we see a Statue of Constantine which was found at the Quirinal; a poor statue, showing the decadence of art at that time. The bronze doors were taken from the Curia at the Forum, by Alexander VII (1655-1667). The **interior** with a nave and four aisles, has the regular form of a basilica; little that is old or medieval remains. The old columns of granite were covered by pilasters by Borromini. The frescoes that decorate the nave are by Muratori and other mannerist painters. The statues of the Apostles all around the nave are of the school of Bernini. The bas-reliefs are among the most important works of Algardi (1603-54), the Caracci of sculpture. The ceiling is the superb work of F. Boulanger and Vico di Raffaele. The pavement is cosmatesque. Underneath it were found notable remains of ancient constructions.

Leo XIII ordered the architect Vespignani to extend the apse. The transfer of the * **Mosaic of the Redeemer** was ably executed and this venerable work was also restored. Under the reign of Constantine the Great, amidst the enthusiasm of the people, the great Basilica of the Saviour was inaugurated with solemn ceremonies and after three centuries of ferocious persecutions, Christianity was declared the religion of the Empire. At that moment the Figure of the Redeemer, smiling and blessing the people, appeared from the apse, thus sanctioning the sublime rite with His divine presence. This is the subject of the mosaic that was made a few years later, many centuries before Jacopo Torriti with the aid of Jacopo da Camerino, restored it in 1291: the most precious and venerated mosaic in Rome.

The magnificent choir, rich in all kinds of marbles, with two powerful organs, can compare with the best works of the Imperial era. In the centre of the transept the **Papal Altar** is surmounted by a canopy, upheld by four columns erected in 1367 by Urban V (1362-70). Below, in the Confessional, there is a bronze tablet, a fine work of Simone, brother of Donatello. It bears the reclining figure of Martin V, a good Pope, who in the inscription is called: « temporum suorum felicitas » (joy of his time).

To the left of the Tribune, the splendid **Monument to Leo XIII**, noble work of Tadolini. Leo XIII, one of the greatest modern Popes, was buried here in October 1924. In this monument, Tadolini combined the Renaissance style with the modern. The statue at left, a workman, reminds us of the encyclical "Rerum Novarum" that was called the Magna Charta of Christian Sociology, in which Leo established the reciprocal relations between workers and employers in the practice of justice and love.

THE HOLY STAIRCASE. Tradition has it that Jesus climbed this staircase in the house of Pontius Pilate. The staircase was later brought to Rome by the pious Empress Helen, mother of Constantine the Great.

Near the altar of the Sacrament is the entrance to the cosmatesque **Cloister** made by Vassalletto and his sons. It is without doubt the most exquisite type of this kind of architecture rivaling the over-restored one in the Basilica of St. Paul outside the Walls.

Right in front of the façade of the Basilica, since 1926, is the bronze **Statue of St. Francis,** who raises his arms towards the Lateran Church as he really must have done in front of the Patriarchium when he first met the Pope who ruled the Catholic World. Thus did Innocent III see him in a dream sustaining the imperilled Lateran.

LATERAN. The papal altar, sheltered under a canopy, was erected by Urban V. in 1367. ►

The square known as CAMPO DE' FIORI was for a long time the place where capital punishments were carried out. Today it is one of Rome's most colourful and busy markets.

fifth itinerary

LARGO ARGENTINA
CAMPO DE' FIORI
JANICULUM
ST. PETER IN MONTORIO

The **Fountain of the Tortoises** in the small Piazza Mattei, is the most charming in Rome. Its beauty and its fine lines gave birth to the legend that this artistic jewel of the late 16th century was designed by Raphael; in reality, it is the work of Landini (1585).

Four Republican Temples not impressive in size but interesting and very ancient, have come to light in the monumental zone of largo Torre Argentina.

S. Andrea della Valle was constructed, on the design of C. Maderno, from 1591 to 1650. The dome, the highest in Rome after St. Peter's, is also one of the finest. The façade of travertine is an imposing work by Rainaldi.

The interior forms a Latin cross. The ample nave, wide, beautiful and full of light, the large side chapels, the apse, the ceiling and dome all combine to give an impression of splendour and solemnity.

The **Campo de' Fiori** is the place where for a long time capital punishment took place. Here on February 17th 1600, the philosopher Giordano Bruno, who escaped punishment in Switzerland, Bohemia and England, was burned as a heretic. The monument is the fine work of Ettore Ferrari (1887).

And now, after crossing the Ponte Amedeo di Savoia, we go up to the **JANICULUM,** from where a most varied and attractive view of the Eternal City is obtained. At the end of the slope of Sant'Onofrio we enter the villa, where the beautiful « Passeggiata of the Gianicolo » running all round the hill, begins.

On the right, in the **Church of St. Onophrius,** stands the Monument to Torquato Tasso, a work by De Fabris, erected by order of Pope Pius IX two centuries and a half after the poet's death.

In the adjoining convent, Tasso lived for some time waiting for the day of his coronation at the Capitol. But on April 25th, 1595, on the eve of his triumph, he died.

Proceeding along the slope, amid a group of cypresses we come across the historical ruin of **Tasso's oak,** beneath which the poet loved to sit in the shade and where San Filippo Neri gathered many young boys in order to teach them by amusing them.

Further on, we reach the **Lighthouse,** a symbol of the Italian spirit of Rome; from its small terrace we admire the first panorama of the « passeggiata ».

Still further, on the left, there is the 16th century **Lante Pavillion** and on the right we see the **Monument to Anita Garibaldi,** a splendid work by M. Rutelli (1932). Still further we reach the large terrace of the Gianicolo on which stands the **Monument to Giuseppe Garibaldi,** a work by E. Gallori (1895).

It is from this terrace that one has the most famous view of the City.

On the distant horizon we see a semicircle of very familiar mountains, looking like a huge

The best view of the city is enjoyed from the JANICULINE HILL.

Greek theatre. Between these mountains and the city, there stretches the country, across which the armies of many nations have passed, in different epochs and for many different causes. The Passeggiata Gianicolense ends in the beautiful avenue bordered by the busts of the patriots of the Roman Republic (1849). On the right of the exit, we see the **Fontana Paolina,** the most splendid water work in Rome, made by G. Fontana and C. Maderno, erected in 1611 by Paul V who restored the aqueduct constructed by Trajan in the year 109 in order to carry the water from Bracciano Lake to Rome.

Further down, on the left, we come to the church of **San Pietro in Montorio** where Beatrice Cenci (1577-1599) famous for her tragic history, was buried. She was arrested with other members of her family and on September 11th, 1599 they were all executed.

The famous Renaissance architect Bramante erected his glorius **Tempietto** in the courtyard of the convent, on the spot where, according to one tradition, St. Peter was crucified.

The TORTOISE FOUNTAIN, one of the many beautiful Baroque fountains to be found in Rome, was ► designed by Giacomo della Porta and executed by the sculptor Taddeo Landini in 1585.

The monumental TREVI FOUNTAIN, another example of the Baroque style, was constructed by Nicolò Salvi under the pontificate of Clement XII. in 1762. He based himself on designs by Alberti and Bernini.

sixth itinerary

TREVI FOUNTAIN
TRINITA' DEI MONTI
VILLA BORGHESE
FORO ITALICO

The **via del Corso** is the principal, most central, and most typical of the old Roman streets. At one end of its narrow but imposingly straight line, nearly a mile long, is the obelisk of the Piazza del Popolo; at the other end, the « Vittoriano ». It is bordered with many papal and princely palaces (Salviati, Odescalchi, Sciarra, Marignoli, on the right; Bonaparte, Doria, Chigi, Fiano, Ruspoli, Rondanini, on the left). The name Corso (race) derived from the special horse races that took place there up to the past century: it replaced the ancient « via Lata ».

To the right of the Via del Corso, in the Via delle Muratte, is the most sumptuous fountain in Rome:

The **FONTANA DI TREVI** is not only celebrated for its excellent water but for the legend that whoever drinks it or throws a coin in the fountain, will assure his return to Rome. It is the façade of a large palace decorated with statues and bas-reliefs on heaps of rocks: the water gushes from every part. It was Agrippa who brought the Virgin Water to Rome by means of an aqueduct. The fountain was built by the architect Salvi (1735) in the time of Clement XII, and decorated by several artists of Bernini's school.

It is said that the soldiers of Agrippa, looking for water in the via Collatina in the country, met a maiden who showed them the source of this pure water, which was hence called Virgin Water. The bas-relief on the right represents this event; that on the left shows Agrippa explaining to Augustus the plan to bring this water to Rome.

Almost at the centre of the Corso is the **Piazza Colonna,** with the Column of Marcus Aurelius. After the death of the Emperor-Philosopher, the Senate erected a temple and a column in his honour. The column was surmounted by a bronze statue of the Emperor.

Behind the Palazzo Chigi is the **House of Parliament; t**he old part, the Innocenziano Palace was built by Bernini and the new one by Basile. Continuing, we come to the Largo Goldoni. From here, by the Via Condotti, we reach the **PIAZZA DI SPAGNA.** The first thing that strikes us are the charming * **Monumental Steps** (1722). At the top of these, the church of **SS. Trinità dei Monti** with two cupolas (1495). An obelisk, found in the gardens of Sallust in 1808, rises in front of the church.

In the interior of the church, the masterpiece of Daniele da Volterra, the famous fresco of the Descent from the Cross.

At the foot of the steps, prettily lies the fine Fountain of the « **Barcaccia** » by Pietro Bernini, father of the famous sculptor and architect Gian Lorenzo. To the right, in the nearby Piazza Mignanelli, in front of the Propaganda Fide Palace, rises the **Column** of the Immaculate Conception erected to commemorate the proclamation of this Dogma.

The TREVI FOUNTAIN and its rustling water animate a small square in the centre of Rome, a jewel of 18th century architecture that suddenly and surprisingly presents itself to the visitor's eyes after he has traversed a series of tiny, narrow streets.

The **PIAZZA DEL POPOLO** was designed by Valadier at the beginning of the last century. In the centre stands the second **obelisk** of the city, brought to Rome by Augustus and raised here by Fontana at the time of Sixtus V. It is a vast square, architecturally superb and simmetrically perfect.

The ashes of Nero were placed by the faithful hands of Acte into the tomb of the Domiti family. The legend says that in early medieval days the spirit of Nero troubled the place and for this reason, the people destroyed the Mausoleum and built a church: **S. Maria « del Popolo »** (derived from latin « Populus » that is popular) one of the most interesting in Rome, a real museum of the Renaissance.

Among the many works of art to be seen here are: **Adoration of the Child,** by Pinturicchio on the altar of the first chapel on the right; a **Tabernacle by Andrea Bregno,** in the Sacristy; two monuments by Sansovino: to Cardinal della Rovere, on the right, and to Cardinal Sforza, on the left of the high altar. On the ceiling, the **Coronation of the Virgin** and other frescoes by Pinturicchio; two masterpieces by Caravaggio: **Saul on the road to Damascus,** on one side, the **Crucifixion of St. Peter,** on the other, in a chapel of the transept on the left. Martin Luther, then an Augustinian friar, lived in the adjoining convent.

VIA CONDOTTI, a narrow street that leads from Via del Corso to Piazza di Spagna(in the background), is undoubtedly one of the most elegant and sophisticated thoroughfares in the city. ►

As soon as one arrives in PIAZZA DI SPAGNA one is struck by the enchanting staircase that leads up to the CHURCH OF TRINITA' DEI MONTI. In springtime the staircase gives hospitality to an exhibition of azaleas and it then becomes a splendid sea of colour.

The Garden of the **PINCIO,** created by Valadier, is the most beautiful and elegant of the city. There is a wonderful view from the high terrace: in the distance St. Peter's and the Vatican dominated by the Dome of Michelangelo, the largest one ever built, in the most brilliant sky. People come here to admire the famous Roman sunsets.

Now we enter one of the loveliest gardens of Rome: a revelation of what Rome and the greatness of the nobility could do jointly: a garden not to be found elsewhere: the **VILLA BORGHESE.** After the election of Paul V, a Borghese, his young nephew, Scipio, was made Cardinal with a very substantial prebend. The Cardinal ordered Van Zans to design this splendid Villa, a Paradise of delight, as it was called at the time.

On the highest point of the Villa stands the Borghese Pavillion. It was built in 1613 by the

The CHURCH OF TRINITA' DEI MONTI was erected in 1495 by commission of the French government ▶ and intended for the use of French Catholics.

The romantic **LAKE IN THE VILLA BORGHESE PARK** with its small temple once dedicated to Aesculapius.

Dutch architect van Zans (Vasanzio) and restored in 1782 by order of Marcantonio Borghese. Today it is the home of the **BORGHESE MUSEUM AND GALLERY.**

The same Cardinal Scipione Borghese kept his extremely rich collections of works of art, both sculptures and paintings, in this Pavillion. Towards the end of the 17th century the best pictures were taken from the gallery to the Borghese Palace. One century after this, the museum that in the meantime had been again enriched by Marcantonio Borghese, with new classical sculptures, had to suffer a still more severe spoliation by Camillo Borghese who, being a brother in-law of Napoleon, ceded a large part of his works of art to the Louvre in Paris. The protests of the Papal government were all in vain, and it was necessary to collect new statues and marbles with which Francesco Borghese succeeded in bringing the

A characteristic corner of the STAIRCASE OF TRINITA' DEI MONTI, a meeting place for young people of every race.

The view from the terrace on the Pincine Hill. The foreground is occupied by PIAZZA DEL POPOLO.

The gracious MOSES FOUNTAIN on the Pincine Hill.   The CLOCK FOUNTAIN on the Pincine Hill. ►

museum to its present state.

Leaving Villa Borghese by Piazzale Flaminio, we admire the **Porta del Popolo** that recalls the entry of Charles V (1536) and of Christine of Sweden. Following via Flaminia we reach **Ponte Milvio,** site of the battle between Maxentius and Constantine, whence the latter, having defeated his enemy, moved triumphantly towards Rome, on the 28th of October 312.

Following the Tiber, to the left, in front of the new Duca d'Aosta Bridge, rises the very modern **FORO ITALICO,** a group of stadium and buildings for sports. We note in the centre of the outer square the Monolith, and obelisk made of a single block of Carrara marble, 55 feet tall.

In the building to the left there is a big swimming-pool; at the back of the inner square, the Fountain of the Globe, with an enormous sphere of marble surrounded by a circular spray of water. To the left, the Stadium with sixty marble statues symbolizing various athletic games. To the left, the immense Olympic Stadium, capable of holding 100.000 spectators.

The OLYMPIC STADIUM is the largest of its kind in Italy; it can accommodate about 100,000 spectators.

MINERVA
PANTHEON
NAVONA SQUARE
ST. ANGEL CASTLE

S. MARIA SOPRA MINERVA, the only large Gothic church in Rome, was designed by the Dominican friars who built S. Maria Novella in Florence (1280-1290) and is a real museum of art and history.

Under the high altar, in a marble sarcophagus lies the **Body of St. Catherine of Siena** (1347-1380). Her greatest glory consists in having persuaded the Pope to return to Rome, after the « Babylonian captivity » of the Church had lasted seventy three years. Dante, Petrarch, and many other good Italians attempted it but their efforts were fruitless. Young Catherine tried first by correspondence, then went to Avignon. Gregory XI returned to Rome. Her letters to Kings, Popes and other important people, are of great political importance, and their spirituality and literary value place her on the level of Dante and Petrarch.

To the left of the altar is the **Statue of Christ,** designed by Michelangelo but finished by his pupils (1514-1521), which shows Christ as seen by St. Peter on the Appian Way, according to a pious legend.

The **obelisk of Minerva,** in the square of the same name, stood originally in front of the temple of Isis. It was put here by order of Alexander VII in 1667. Bernini whimsically set the obelisk on the back of an elephant, a work of Ferrata, one of his best pupils.

The **PANTHEON,** a glory of the Eternal City, is the most perfect of all classical monuments in Rome. The inscription on the architrave of the portico « M. Agrippa L. F. Cos tertium fecit » refers to a temple erected by Agrippa in 27 B.C. to the tutelary divinities of the Julia family. For a long time, it was thought that the Pantheon, as it is today, was the original temple of Agrippa. In reality Agrippa's building was destroyed by a great fire in A.D. 80. Recent studies have proved that the present Pantheon is a reconstruction of the time of Hadrian. Other alterations were made at the time of Septimius Severus and of Caracalla.

On the 6th March 609, Boniface IV, with the permission of Emperor Phocas, changed the pagan temple into a Christian church dedicating it to **St. Mary of the Martyrs.** It is to this fact we owe the preservation of the Pantheon. The bodies of many martyrs were removed from the Catacombs to be buried here.

As a sanctuary, in virtue of the Lateran Pact, it acquired the status of palatine basilica or, in other words, of the national church of all Italians, a novelty which appears for the first time in the history of Italy.

The **portico** is supported by 16 monolithic granite columns; in the tympanum there was a bas-relief in bronze representing the battle of gods and giants. The ceiling of the portico was covered with bronze. This precious material, weighing about 450.000 lbs, was removed by order of Urban VIII (1623-1644) and used

The PANTHEON, one of the most famous monuments of ancient Rome, was erected by Agrippa in 27 A.D.

by Bernini for the high altar at St. Peter's and other works. In the two niches were the statues of Augustus and Agrippa. The bronze doors are original.

The height and diameter of the interior are equal, both being 142 feet. Light and air enter through an opening 30 feet wide in the centre of the dome. The world has nothing to equal it. The majestic **dome** with its opening showing the sky which seems to descend into the temple, left open so that prayer could freely ascend, gives us an impression of solemnity that not even St. Peter's can produce. Its simple regularity, the beauty of its parts and the splendid material give the interior a sublime character. All around are seven niches. In the centre stood the statue of Jove Ultor who punished the assassins of Caesar; in the others were statues of the chief divinities. Other gods and heroes were in the intermediary spaces. Only the splendid columns of antique yellow marble remain to give us an idea of its primitive splendour.

Sovereigns and artists have their tombs in the Pantheon: In the first chapel to the left repose the remains of **Perin del Vaga** (1500-1547), con-

The MINERVA OBELISK, which we here see in the small square in front of the Church of S. Maria sopra Minerva, was designed by Bernini and executed by Ferrata in 1667. ▶

sidered second only to Giulio Romano among Raphael's pupils.

Next is the **tomb of Baldassarre Peruzzi** (1481-1536), a great painter and architect.

In the second chapel are the **tombs of King Humbert I** and **Queen Margherita.**

Between the second and third chapels, the tomb that contains the earthly remains of Raphael, one of the most popular artists in the world, whose epigraph says: « Living, great Nature feared he might outlive her works; and dying, fears herself to die ». The **Statue of the Madonna** is the work of his pupil Lorenzetto.

Close by is the **tomb of Maria Bibbiena,** his promised wife, who died three months before him. Above is the **tomb of Annibale Caracci.** In the third chapel we see the **Cenotaph of Cardinal Consalvi** (1755-1824) an exquisite work by Thorwaldsen.

In the sixth chapel, is the **tomb of Victor Emanuel II.** On the altar of the seventh chapel, a fresco of the **Annunciation,** by Melozzo da Forlì.

The **PIAZZA NAVONA,** or Circo Agonale, occupies the place of the Stadium of Domitian, that could hold 30.000 spectators. Here are three magnificent fountains. The one in the centre

The **INSIDE OF THE PANTHEON** has a diameter of 43.40 metres (about 143 ft) and is as high again. Some of Italy's most famous kings and artist are buried here.

The PANTHEON is the most perfectly preserved of all the classical monuments that have survived in Rome. With the permission of the Byzantine Emperor Foca, Pope Boniface IV. converted the pagan temple into a Christian church in 609 and used it as a resting place for the bodies of Christian martyrs transferred here from the catacombs.

PIAZZA NAVONA is one of the largest squares in Rome. It stands above the remains of the Circus of Domitian whose original form it preserves.

« an Aesop's fable in marble » is the famous **Fountain of Rivers** by Bernini, who made a fanciful pedestal for the Egyptian obelisk that used to stand in the Circus of Maxentius.

It contains four statues which represent the Danube, the Ganges, the Nile and the Rio de la Plata.

The church of **S. Agnese in Agone,** is built on the spot where, according to tradition, the virgin, denuded before her martyrdom, was man-tled in her hair, which had grown miraculously to cover her. It is a magnificent Baroque building designed by G. Rainaldi and Borromini. Underneath it there are some remains of the original church and of the Circus of Domitian.

CASTEL SANT'ANGELO. Artemisia, Queen of Halicarnassus, wife of King Mausolus, became immortal through the magnificent tomb, one of the wonders of the world, which she erected for her husband. It was called Mausoleum, and

◄ This STATUE OF CHRIST, sculptured by Michelangelo, can be seen in the Church of S. Maria sopra Minerva where it stands to the left of the principal altar.

PIAZZA NAVONA. The FOUNTAIN OF THE FOUR RIVERS (seen by night) is the work of Bernini. Four figures represent the Danube, the Ganges, the Nile and the River Plate.

this name has been used ever since for tombs of large dimensions. The **Mausoleum of Hadrian** surpassed in dimensions and magnificence every other tomb. We get no idea of it from what remains. It would require too great an effort of imagination to reconstruct the majestic edifice. Procopius, the Byzantine historian of the 6th century, left us a description of it in his time. The Mausoleum had square foundations above which rose a big tower adorned with Doric columns, statues and spaces for epitaphs of the dead. On the top was a colossal group representing Hadrian in a chariot drawn by four

horses. All the enormously thick walls were faced with Parian marble. It was, after the Colosseum, the most splendid example of Roman architecture.

At the death of the Emperor, the Mausoleum was not yet finished; his successor Antoninus Pius brought his remains to Rome. His successors and princes of Imperial families were buried here up to Caracalla. The history of Hadrian's Mausoleum follows the history of Rome and both saw the struggles and treachery of the Middle Ages, the splendour of the Papal Court in the Renaissance, the horrors of the

The FOUNTAIN OF THE FOUR RIVERS in Piazza NAVONA, below its tall central obelisk (an Egiptian ► original).

The SANT'ANGELO BRIDGE was constructed by the Emperor Hadrian in 134 to give acces to his MAUSOLEUM. The statues are later additions executed by the school of Bernini.

Sack of Rome in 1527, the furious bombardments during many sieges, and inoffensive fireworks of festivities. Under Aurelian (275) but more probably under Honorius (403) it was strongly fortified and incorporated in the city walls in order to form a real bastion, in defence of the banks of the Tiber. This strategic function came into evidence in the first invasion of the barbarians led by Alaric in 410. We know it had six towers, 164 battlements, 14 platforms for artillery and 18 loopholes. The transformation into a castle propably took place in the 10th century when it fell into the possession of

Alberic and Marotia. Then it passed to the Crescenzi family and in 1277 was occupied by Nicholas III who joined it to St. Peter's by means of the subterranean passage and since then it has remained in the possession of the Popes.

The name **Castel Sant'Angelo** dates from the 12th century but owes its origin to a much older legend. During a solemn procession made in 590 by St. Gregory the Great to implore the Virgin to stop the plague that ravaged the city, an angel appeared in the sky and alighted on the top of the Mausoleum, sheathing his sword as a sign that the prayer was granted. A chapel was then erected in honour of the angel; and later a statue, commemorating the miracle; and the name and attributions of the building were changed.

The castle is steeped in memories of bloodshed and crime. Famous prisoners were shut up in it. Arnaldo da Brescia, ardent adversary of temporal dominion, was accused by St. Bernard of following the doctrines of Peter Abelard; denounced, he had to leave Paris and came to Rome where he began a campaign against the clargy. In July 1148, Eugene III excommunicated Arnaldo and his followers. A cardinal was killed and the Pope placed Rome under an interdict. Arnaldo was burned and his ashes thrown into the Tiber.

Clement VII was besieged in this fort, while the city was occupied by invaders led by the Prince of Orange. From the 6th of May to the 3rd of June 1527, the poor Pope from the corridor of the Castle witnessed the horrible saturnalia of blood and licence, theft and sacrilege, in terrible excesses after the Constable of Bourbon entered the city with his ferocius hordes (Sack of Rome).

Castel S. Angelo · THE COURT-YARD OF THE ANGEL.

A picturesque view of CASTEL SANT'ANGELO.

Benvenuto Cellini, during the siege, rendered great services to Clement VII and he himself speaks of having killed the Bourbon and afterwards Philibert, Prince of Orange. Cellini was imprisoned here and released by the intercession of Cardinal d'Este. Beatrice Cenci was kept here for more than four months. Giuseppe Balsamo, Count of Cagliostro (1743-95), the famous adventurer, who travelled all over Europe selling love philters, elixir of youth, and powders that were to beautify ugly women, implicated in the affair of a diamond necklace in Paris, came to Rome in 1780, and was arrested and imprisoned in the Castle. He ended his days at St. Leo.

The **Ponte S. Angelo** was built by Hadrian as an approach to his mausoleum. It is decorated with beautiful figures of angels, designed by Gian Lorenzo Bernini and accomplished by his pupils.

eighth itinerary

BATH OF CARACALLA
APPIAN WAY
CATACOMBS
CLAUDIAN AQUEDUCT

No other road is so well known, in the world as the **Via Appia.** Proudly called the « Regina Viarum », it was begun by Appius Claudius in 312 B.C. Bordering it for many miles, were sepulchres and tomb-stones of twenty generations. Only patrician families could have tombs here. Here were the tombs of the Scipios, Furii, Manili, Sestili.

The first part of the Appian Way is called Via Porta San Sebastiano. At the beginning, the famous **Baths of Caracalla** or Antonine Baths, begun by Septimius Severus in 206 and inaugurated in 217 by Caracalla, although finished by his successors Heliogabal and Alexander Severus. Sixteen hundred persons could bathe here at the same time. So vast were the baths that to the eyes of Ammianus Marcellinus they seemed like provinces. There were rooms for cold, hot and warm baths, splendid ceilings, porticoes, pillared halls, gymnasiums, where the rarest marbles, the most colossal columns, the finest statues were admired by the people; even the baths were of basalt, granite, alabaster.

Today, in this suggestive and inimitable setting of imposing ruins, there is the greatest open-air Opera in Europe.

Before passing the Porta Appia or Porta San Sebastiano, we see the so-called **Arch of Drusus.**

Drusus (38-8 B.C.), second son of Livia, one of the most distinguished men of his time, took command of the legions against the free tribes of the Eastern Alps.

« Strike once and not twice » was the order given by Augustus; and these tribes did not appear again for a thousand years. Some of the most valiant Raeti are remembered in the martial Ode of Horace: « Videre Raeti ».

He was the first Roman general who reached the North Sea and was nicknamed Germanicus. He died in Germany and his ashes were placed in the Mausoleum of Augustus. The **Porta San Sebastiano** (former Porta Appia) is in the Aurelian Wall, begun by Aurelius in 272, finished by Probus in 279. It is well preserved.

One of the most celebrated spots on the Via Appia is **Quo Vadis?** where, according to a religious legend, Peter had vision of Christ.

Nero persecuted the Christians to calm the fury of the people against him for the burning of Rome. St. Peter was asked by the Christians to leave Rome for a while until the persecution was over. He consented; but not far from Porta Appia, he met a traveller going towards Rome. Peter had seen Him before. He recognized His face, His figure. He had heard Him preach, had seen Him die, rise again, ascend to Heaven. « Domine, quo vadis? » (Master, where goest Thou?) Peter stammered trembling. The

The OLD APPIAN HIGHWAY, often called "Queen of the Roads", is one of the most famous of all Roman roads. It was constructed by Appius Claudius in 312 B.C.

other replied: « I am going to Rome to be crucified again ». The vision vanished but the divine footprints remained on a paving stone. This is the sublime legend recorded by Origen (254).

In front of the chapel of Quo Vadis, is the circular ruin of the **Tomb of Priscilla,** one of the few identified tombs on the Appian Way. Priscilla was the beloved wife of Abascantius, a favorite freed-man of Domitian. She died young. Her husband erected a splendid monument. Statius (45-96), the best poet of those days, wrote a letter of condolence to the best of husbands on the loss of his beloved Priscilla: « It is a pleasure to love a wife when living, it is religion to love her when she is dead », where he describes the sorrow of the husband, the funeral and the splendid tomb decorated with rich marbles and statues. « Centuries will pass but no force can ever destroy this tomb »; the poet had not foreseen the fury and devastation of war.

The underground Christian cemeteries are still known by the name of **Catacombs.** This name, erroneously used, originally served to indicate the locality underneath the present Basilica of

Before passing through St. Sebastian's Gate, we encounter the so-called ARCH OF DRUSUS which ► dates back to the 2nd century B.C.

St. Sebastian, where the ground sloped down towards an excavation of pozzolana earth called « in catacumbas ».

Formerly in Rome, the areas destined by the Christians for burials, were called « Coemeteria », a place of rest. It seems that at Naples, in the 9th century, the name catacomb was given for the first time to an old underground cemetery.

The Catacombs of St. Callixtus and St. Sebastian are the ones most visited by the numerous pilgrimages that come to the Eternal City.

The **Catacombs of St. Callixtus** show us the first Christian cemetery of the Christian Community in Rome, to administer which Pope Zephyrinus (199-217) chose the deacon Callixtus, who was later Pope from 217 to 222. The Salesians are now their custodians.

The **Catacombs of St. Sebastian** (over which since the 4th century is a magnificent basilica in honour of the Apostles Peter and Paul), received the precious relic of the martyr of the same name.

The excavations begun in 1915 and continuing today, have brought to light a particularly important series of buildings, delicated to the memory of the two Apostles up to the third century. It may justly be said that they form the most important monument of underground Christian Rome. The Franciscans are the custodians of these Catacombs.

The **Catacombs of Domitilla** — an imposing collection of catacombs and burial grounds — are a true Christian necropolis, originating in the underground chamber of the Flavi, where the martyr St. Domitilla, the niece of Domitian, was buried together with the two praetorians, St. Nereo and St. Achilles, and St. Petronilla, who legend says was the daughter of the apostle St. Peter.

The remarkable basilica, with its three naves, lit from above, and — on several levels connected by staircases — a vast network of endless galleries flanked by a succession of tombs and crypts, cubicles and columbaria, arcosolia and sarcophagi, halls and ambulatories decorated with frescoes in the Pompeian style, sculptures and base-reliefs, architectural motifs and epigraphs dating from the second century, all combine to make these catacombs not only the largest but also one of the most interesting underground complexes in Rome. They are in the care of the Friars of Mercy.

The **Tomb of Romulus** was erected by Maxentius who also constructed the splendid circus that bears his name.

The **Tomb of Cecilia Metella** rises solemnly on a height along the via Appia. Cecilia was the daughter of Metellus Creticus and wife of Crassus. The tomb still bears an inscription. In the Middle Ages, the Caetani family changed the tomb into a fortress and erected a castle around it.

The Roman Country, whose profound beauty not all understand, should be seen late in the afternoon, at sunset.

The Campagna was at one time full of patrician tombs, military roads and of villas where noble families lived, of great aqueducts that brought water to the baths and fountains and irrigated the country. Now all this magnificence has disappeared. Among various ruins the arches of the **Claudian Aqueduct** are noteworthy. It was finished by Claudius in 52.

Foto Vis-Color Pazienti

The **TOMB OF CECILIA METELLA** on the Old Appian Highway is a sepulchral monument dedicated to the daughter of Metellus Creticus. It has a diameter of 20 metres. The Caetani Family transformed it into a fortress in 1302; the battlemented walls can still be seen today

THE VATICAN CITY

The **VATICAN** has been the residence of the Popes for about six centuries (since 1377). Before the transfer of the Pontificial Court to Avignon (1309-1377), the Papal see was at the Lateran.

Since that remote epoch it may be said that there has not been a Pope who has not contributed to the grandeur and dignity of this sacred place and made it still more worthy of the Supreme Head of Catholicism and the monarch of a dynasty that considers States and Empires its children. In fact, about 260 Popes have sat on the throne of St. Peter, in an uninterrupted line, many of them martyrs and saints. Their history has been and will always be the history of civilization: the constant struggle of the spirit against matter; of order against disorder; of truth against falsehood; of freedom against slavery. For twenty centuries the history of the Vatican has been the history of the world. Tempest after tempest, generations and centuries have come with their threats and perils: but all these have passed and the Vatican still remains.

Since February 11th, 1929, the Vatican has been an independent State under the name of Vatican City, in virtue of the Lateran Pact by which the Roman Question was definitely resolved.

The body of St. Peter was buried at the Circus Neronianus, where, under Nero, the Apostle was crucified. Over his tomb, Constantine erected a magnificent basilica that in the course of time, became one of the wonders of the world. During the seventy-three years that the Popes were in Avignon, the basilica was so neglected that it was almost impossible to restore it. Nicholas V decided to reconstruct it giving the project to Rossellino. On the death of the Pope, the work was suspended. It was Julius II (1503-1513) who initiated the building of the new Basilica.

Bramante was ordered to make the design and to start the first part of this architectural undertaking, the biggest in the world ever attempted, and which took 176 years to complete. In so many years, architects and designs followed one after the other (Raphael, Sangallo etc.), till Michelangelo, almost seventy years old, adopted Bramante's design of a Greek cross with a dome. After his death, work was continued following the same plan. But at the time of Paul V (1605-21), Maderno finally decided on the design of a Latin cross.

Let us now admire St. Peter's square, in front of the greatest church of Christianity: **ST. PETER'S IN THE VATICAN.**

The **square** is unique. It is dominated by the immense suggestive * **Dome,** by Michelangelo. It is a harmonious poem of immensity. The dome rises gigantic against the background of the sky and its silver-blue colour merges with the same tint of the heavenly dome of which it seems the architectural synthesis. When Mi-

ST. PETER'S SQUARE is by far the largest in Rome. It is 340 metres in length and has a width of 240 metres. A beautiful Egyptian obelisk, 25 metres high, stands at its centre.

chelangelo's immortal genius conceived it, he must have perceived this sense of the absolute and infinite that would impress the soul of whoever saw it. It seems as if the entire world is included in it and all that the human mind has of transcendent, pure, noble, great, and derived from the ascent of civilization, joins the prayers and devoted aspirations of the Christian City, venerating the glorious tomb of the Prince of the Apostles.

The **colonnade** is the finest work of Bernini and forms a superb entry to St. Peter's and the Vatican. The two large wings opening like half circles seem like the two outstretched arms of the temple receiving all mankind in one universale embrace. Nothing more harmonious can be imagined. If Bernini appears extravagant in some of his other works, in this colonnade he has shown all the power of his genius. He

was also the sculptor of the numerous statues that decorate it.

No sight more solemn can be offered to Romans and foreigners than that of the benediction of the immense tightly packed crowd, on a radiant Easter day. A more imposing sight cannot be imagined. The Pontiff, in tiara and mantle is carried on his gestatorial chair to the balcony in the centre of the façade. All the multitude acclaims him and then kneels. The bells, the anthems, the silver trumpets are hushed, and a deep silence fills the square. « Urbs et Orbis » (the city and the world) receive the benediction of the Pope on the bright, happy Christian Easter.

The erection of the **obelisk** roused great wonder and enthusiasm in the people. Sixtus V after conferring with many architects, decided to assign this work to Domenico Fontana. It

ST. PETER'S SQUARE. In the background the building with the windows of the Papal apartments.

was begun on the 3rd of April 1586 and the enormous monolith was raised on September 10th, in the presence of a great crowd, with the aid of nine hundred men.

The **two fountains,** the one on the right, designed by Maderno in 1613, and the one on the left, in 1675 by Bernini, harmonize perfectly with the vast square.

The **façade** was designed by Maderno. The name and title of Paul V Borghese is written in cubital letters.

In the **portico,** above the main entrance, is the famous « Navicella » frescoed for the old St. Peter's church by Giotto, during the year of the first Jubilee (1300) and badly restored.

The **bronze door**, designed by Filarete, in imitation of that by Ghiberti at Florence, was also in the old basilica.

The **Porta Santa** (Holy Door) is opened only every twenty-five years. On these occasions on Christmas Eve, the Pope, following a special rite, goes in solemn procession to this

Aerial view of VIA DELLA CONCILIAZIONE.

BERNINI'S FOUNTAIN in St. Peter's Square.

door, and after a triple genuflection and three strokes of a hammer, the wall is removed and the Pope enters first. At the end of the Jubilee year the door is shut with special solemnities. The first door on the left is a work of Manzù (1964), who has there represented Jesus's Ascension and the Virgin's Assumption.

Now let us enter the Church, the imposing sanctuary of Christ built over the body of His Martyr. All the world makes a pilgrimage to it. Pilgrims of every class and nation kneel before this common Sanctuary.

The **high altar,** under the dome of Michelan-gelo, rises over the **tomb of St. Peter.** Ninety five lamps burn day and night before it.

In the **Confessional** is the statue of **Pius VI** kneeling, by Canova. Over the altar, the famous **canopy** of Bernini, upheld by four spiral columns, made with bronze taken from the Pantheon. But the glorification of the tomb of the humble fisherman of Galilee is the majestic **dome** rising up to the sky the multiple choirs of angels and blessed souls around the throne of the Most High in a glory of light, harmony and immensity.

In the niches of the colossal pillars are four

The majestic DOME OF ST. PETER'S, the work of Michelangelo, is 136 metres high and has a diameter ▶ of 42 metres.

THE MANZU' GATE

The INTERIOR OF THE BASILICA OF ST. PETER leaves us openmouthed by virtue of its immense size. The central nave is 186 metres long and 46 metres high.

statues: St. Andrew, by Duquesnoy; St. Veronica, by Mochi; St. Helena, by Bolgi; St. Longinus, by Bernini.

On the right of the pillar of St. Longinus, seated on a throne, is the celebrated **bronze statue of St. Peter.**

Now let us start the tour of the basilica.

In the first chapel of the right aisle above the altar, we admire the *Pietà, one of the most beautiful works of young Michelangelo. The name of the young artist is chiseled on the sash that goes over the Madonna's shoulder. On the knees of the immortally young Virgin lies the body of Christ who seems asleep. The Olympian severity of their beautiful figures is surrounded by a veil of sadness.

In the **Tribune,** four Doctors of the Church sustain the papal **see of St. Peter's,** work of genius by Bernini.

St. Peter's Basilica is particularly attractive to tourists visiting Rome, on account of ist magnificence and grandeur for which it is famous all over the world. However, while the impression that one receives from its outside and particularly form the « piazza » and the « cupola » (dome), agrees with one's expectation, the first impression that one gets from the interior of this Temple, especially as regards its size, leaves

105

one rather disappointed. Little by little, though, we change our opinion, while proceeding to visit it (It would be better to make several visits) and we are filled with wonder. This huge building reveals itself as a succession of majestic halls each of which looks almost like a large cathedral. The figures are eloquent: The length of the interior of the Basilica, as revealed by a writing traced on the floor near the bronze gate, is 691 feet. (The outside length including the porch is 694 feet). There follow more writings indicating the length of the largest churches in the world. The vault is 144 feet high. An arcade of the central nave is 75 feet (nearly equal to the obelisk of the square). The dome, inside, is 390 feet high; the lantern is over 55 feet high. Its diameter is 137 feet nearly equal to that of the Pantheon (142), which however, is less high.

The perimeter of each of the four pillars supporting the dome, is 232 feet. The statues in the respective niches are over 16 feet tall. The pen of the Evangelist St. Mark, in the medaillon above the pillar of St. Helena, is 5 ft. high! The canopy is 95 ft., over 13 feet higher than the obelisk.

And if the Church is observed from above (for instance from the interior rail of the dome), one feels really giddy.

THE VATICAN LIBRARY

The **Vatican Library** is the foremost in Europe for the number of antique manuscripts and rare books. It is not possible to calculate the value of this priceless collection. In the sumptuous

THE TOMB OF ST. PETER.

MICHELANGELO'S PIETA'.

BASES · PILARVM

EX · LAPIDE · TIBVRTINO · MARMOREAE

IX · PONTIFICATVS · AN · XIII ·

Bernini's **HOLY WATER STOUP** in St. Peter's.

Sixtine Hall are visible many rare manuscripts such as the Codex of the Bible of the 4th century, four copies of Virgil dating from the third to the fifth centuries, the Gospel of St. Matthew of the sixth century, the famous Palimpsest containing a large part of De Republica by Cicero. This original handwriting of the fourth century was erased on the manuscript in the seventh century to write in its place the commentary « Super Psalmos » by St. Augustine, but was finally rediscovered by Cardinal Angelo Mai.

Along the Gallery are ranged beautiful gifts given to Pius IX, Leo XIII and Pius X by sovereigns and Catholic Associations.

At the end of the Library, in a room to the right, there is a precious collection of antique frescoes, among which the most important represents the **Aldobrandini Nuptials,** found in 1607. It is a pretty composition, part of a long frieze around a room, belonging to the first years of Augustus' reign.

As soon as Raphael came to Rome, he was presented to the Pope Julius II by Bramante. Some rooms above the Borgia apartment had already been frescoed by Perugino, Sodoma

Bernini's famous **CANOPY** covering the papal altar. ►
It was commissioned by Pope Urban VIII.

The CHAIR OF ST. PETER in its masterful setting by Bernini.

The inside of the Dome of St. Peter's (Michelangelo). ►

and others, but Julius II decided to have them scraped and painted again by the young Raphael.

The **first room,** called the room of the **Fire in the Borgo,** was painted at the time of Leo X and it is the last room that Raphael saw finished. The principal fresco represents a fire in the Leonine City (i e: Rome), miraculously extinguished by Leo IV, who made the sign of the cross from a window of the Vatican. In the background is seen the façade of the old church of St. Peter's not yet demolished. The group on the left is noteworthy for its vigorous and powerful design. The motive is taken from Virgil's Fire of Troy: Aeneas, a fine nude figure, fleeing from the fire, carries Anchises on his back and holds Ascanius by the hand. The female figures are drawn with grace and dramatic power.

In 846 the **Saracens** landed at Ostia and sacked the churches of St. Peter and of St. Paul, carrying off the most precious treasures. Three years later, they returned but were defeated in a naval battle. This subject, designed by Raphael, was painted by his pupils. It is a noble composition. The figure of Leo IV is the portrait of Leo X.

The **Coronation of Charlemagne** (800) is so inferior in its composition as to make us doubt that Raphael designed it.

In the **second room** is the first work done by Raphael: the **Dispute of the Holy Sacrament,** finished in 1509. The subject of this magnificent fresco is the glory of the Eucharist, but could be more exactly called the glorification of Catholicism. The figure of Christ above, and the monstrance with the Host below, indicate His double presence, in heaven and on earth.

In the front of the Dispute is the so-called **School of Athens.** Its subject is Human Science, represented by an assembly of great

◀ The bronze STATUE OF ST. PETER. It is generally attributed to Arnolfo di Cambio is here seen in full adornment during a religious ceremony.

The VATICAN LIBRARY, foremost in Europe both on account of its age and its treasures of manuscripts and rare books.

PANORAMIC VIEW FROM THE DOME OF ST. PETER'S.

philosophers of old times: a group arranged with great ability and including the entire philosophical school of Dante.

Above the window we admire **Parnasus.** Around Apollo, playing the lyre, are the Muses and the most celebrated poets, amongst whom are Dante and Petrarch. It has been called: « the most beautiful scene of society ever made ».

Over the other window are the **Three Cardinal Virtues.** To the left, the Emperor Justinian presents his code to Trebonian. This fresco was painted by Raphael's pupils. To the right, Gregory IX (a fine portrait of Julius II) gives the decrees to a lawyer. This fresco shows the influence of Melozzo da Forlì.

The four medallions of the ceiling represent Theology, Philosophy, Poetry and Justice. All the decorative works are designed and executed in a masterly manner.

Heliodorus' room, the third, was painted in 1511-1514; it is so called from the fresco that represents the **chastisement of Heliodorus.** Above the window is the scene of the **Miracle of Bolsena** (1264) when the real presence of Christ in the Eucharist was proved by a surprising miracle to a doubting priest: spots of blood appeared on the Corporal. The Cathedral of Orvieto, an admirable example of Gothic architecture was erected to preserve this Corporal. Julius II, on visiting Orvieto, made a vow before the sacred relic and ordered Raphael to paint this fresco. The Pope is kneeling before the altar. It is a magnificent portrait. In the group of Papal guards every face is an accurate portrayal of marvellous expression and strength, as is also the beautiful group of women and children to the left.

The **Liberation of St. Peter** from prison was painted in 1514. It was arranged around the window with great ability. The three different qualities of light, the moonlight, the splendour of the angel, and the torch-light of the soldiers, are finely portrayed. This fresco contains another political allusion: the liberation of the Church from its French and German enemies.

The **Meeting of Attila** is another allusion to the quarrel with France. The work, begun under Julius II, was finished after his death in 1513. Here we see his successor Leo X appear twice, once as Cardinal and then as Pope. The greater part of this fresco is the work of Raphael's pupils.

In the **last room** is represented the **legendary life of Constantine**. None of the figures were painted by Raphael because he had only finished the design at the time of his death.

The first fresco represents the **Apparition of the Cross** with the inscription « In hoc signo vinces ». (In this sign you will win).

Ceremonial swearing in of the SWISS GUARDS in St. Anne's Courtyard.

THE SIXTINE CHAPEL

ILLUSTRATIONS:

The **Sixtine Chapel** was built by the architect Giovanni de Dolci for Sixtus IV in 1473. The frescoes that decorate it were begun in 1481. They were to represent the Life of Moses (Old Testament) on one side and the Life of Christ (New Testament) on the other, as was the custom in old churches.

The succession of these paintings in the two side walls is therefore parallel. Almost every fresco, in fact, is connected with the one opposite. As it is interesting to compare them, we prefer to proceed alternating from one wall to the other.

The first two frescoes, one on each side, were painted by Pinturicchio.

1. The **Circumcision.** An Angel with his sword stops Moses because he had neglected to circumcise his sons. Zipporah perfoms the ceremony. This group is especially fine and recalls the grace of Raphael; the heads, some of them portraits, are painted with the greatest ability. The panorama is enchanting.

2. The **Baptism of Christ.** God the Father is above between angels and cherubims; below is a dove, symbol of the Holy Ghost over the head of Christ. At the sides, John the Baptist to the left, the Redeemer to the right.

After Pinturicchio comes Botticelli, with the story of Moses on one side and the Temptation of Christ on the other. Alessandro Filipepi, 1444-1510, (called Botticelli from a nickname given by his first master), worked almost two years on these three frescoes which may be considered his masterpieces, although they are not so well known as his works in Florence.

3. The **Story of Moses.** There are various episodes of his youth. In the centre, he draws water for the daughters of Jethro, having driven away the shepherds and killed the Egyptian; on the left, he guides the Israelites through the desert. These groups are painted with great ability, strength of dramatic action and expression in the principal figures.

4. The **Temptation of Christ,** which is the principal subject, is in the background. On top of a building, Satan tempts Jesus: « If you are the Son of God, throw yourself down ». On the left, he asks Him to change stones to bread; to the right he tempts Him, offering Him all the riches of the world, if He will bow before him and adore him.

The fifth and sixth frescoes were painted by Cosimo Rosselli and Ghirlandaio respectively:

5. The **Crossing of the Red Sea.** Cosimo Rosselli was assisted by Piero di Cosimo in painting this fresco, made to commemorate the great victory of the Papal troops over the Neapolitans at Campomarte.

6. The **Calling of the Apostles** is by Ghirlandaio. We honour this artist as the teacher of Michelangelo. Here he has painted two frescoes, one of which is lost. Christ names Peter and Andrew His apostles. Few frescoes can be compared with this. Although weak in colour, this work shows great method and execution; the panorama is unrivalled. To the right we see the portraits of the Florentine colony in Rome, among whom is Vespucci, the Florentine Ambassador and Giovanni Tornabuoni.

Cosimo Rosselli painted the seventh and eighth frescoes.

7. **God gives Moses the Tablets of the Law,** but he breaks them when he sees the people of Israel in adoration before the golden calf.

8. In the **Sermon on the Mount,** we see only two scenes: the Sermon, and the Healing of the Leper. Among the last group to the left, there are two Knights of Rhodes, Giacomo di Almeida and his brother; above the Portuguese Ambassador, in the centre, Charlotte of Lusignano, exiled Queen of Cyprus and her husband, Luigi di Savoia. In the ninth and tenth frescoes the two great masters of Florence and Perugia are competitors: The Power of the Keys of St. Peter, by Perugino, and the Power of the Rod of

Moses, by Botticelli. It is interesting to compare them. While Botticelli tries to surpass his rival in dramatic action, Perugino expresses calm and elegance.

9. The **Punishment of Korah, Dathan and Abiram,** was suggested to Botticelli by a contemporary event. Andrew Zamomelic, archbishop of Carniola, not having been elevated to the rank of a cardinal, called a council at Basle against the Pope, but was imprisoned and committed suicide.

10. **Christ giving the keys to St. Peter** was painted when Perugino was still young and it is certainly one of his best works. In the background we see two triumphal arches and in the centre an octagonal building.

The **Testament and Death of Moses** remains. This great artist surpassed all his contemporaries in the art of painting the anatomy and movement of the nude. The last fresco, the **Last Supper,** is by Rosselli.

In 1508 Julius II, always ready to undertake new enterprises, ordered young Michelangelo to paint the * **Ceiling of the Sixtine Chapel.** The gigantic task was begun in May 1508 and finished on November 2nd, 1512; twenty-three years later, he began the Last Judgement. The artist was not prepared to paint frescoes. As a youth he had been a pupil of Ghirlandaio's, but later had frequented the school of sculpture that Lorenzo de' Medici had opened in the courtyard of St. Mark's at Florence. Some painters were called from Florence to help him. Bramante had built the scaffolding but Michelangelo refused all help from Florentine painters and put up a new scaffolding. In the work of the ceiling, we have before us a revolutionary architect: the prophets, the sibyls, all the figures are the creation of a titanic sculptor. They are, in painting, what his great Moses is in sculpture. The central part of the ceiling is flat; the arches are painted in perspective. The artist created an architectural frame in which to place his principal subjects.

1. God dividing Light from Darkness.
2. The Creation of the Sun and Moon.
3. God dividing the Earth from the Waters.
4. The Creation of Man, who lies on the ground. The Creator is about to touch him with his finger to give him life and a soul. This fresco alone would suffice to immortalize the artist.
5. The Creation of Eve.
6. The fall of Man, who is expelled from Paradise. In the centre we see the Tree of Knowledge and the coiled serpent with the head of a woman, leaning towards the couple, who are picking the forbidden fruit.
7. The Sacrifice of Noah.
8. The Deluge.
9. The Drunkenness of Noah.

The Prophets and the Sibyls in the triangular space are the biggest figures in this monumental painting. They are all seated and accompanied by angels or genii. They represent: 1. Jonah; 2. The Lybian Sibyl; 3. Daniel; 4. The Cumaean Sibyl; 5. Isaiah; 6. The Delphic Sibyl; 7. Zacharias; 8. Joel; 9. The Erythrean Sibyl; 10. Ezekiel; 11. The Persian Sibyl; 12. Jeremiah.

But where Michelangelo reveals his legendary ability is the ***Last Judgement,** full of the spirit of God who creates and destroys, the most perfect work of his long and active career. It is unique, inimitable, stupendous and it conquers and dominates us with the splendid audacity of its creator who infused into it all his own strength. Above, turning to the left, is Christ, the implacable Judge, with his right hand raised in condemnation. The words: « Go ye accursed! » are not written but they are felt. The Madonna at his side appears placidly resigned to the hour of judgement. The others are prophets, apostles, martyrs. On the right of the Messiah are the elect: on the left, the sinners. In heaven, between the lunettes, are the angels with the instruments of His Passion. Below, on the left, the scene of the Resur-

rection of the dead: a group of angels, at the centre, bearing the book of judgment, blow the trumpets while from the open sepulchres the dead come forth to go to the Valley of Jehoshaphat. And while the good rise to Heaven, to the helpless rage of the demons, the evil ones are precipitated into the abyss where Charon with his boat and Minos, the infernal judge, awaits them. The Last Judgement, an epitome of the Divine Comedy and pictorial explosion of the « Dies irae », was begun by Michelangelo in 1535 and finished 1541; six years' work.

The figure of the beautiful poetess, Vittoria Colonna, probably had its influence on the figures of the women in the Last Judgement. Michelangelo fell passionately in love with her.

Paul III, accompanied by his master of ceremonies, Biagio da Cesena, used often to come to see the artist paint, and one day asked Mons. da Cesena his opinion on the work. « Your Holiness, these figures are fit for an inn, not for your chapel ». Michelangelo's only answer was to paint in Biagio da Cesena as Minos. When the master of ceremonies asked to have his portrait removed, Paul III replied: « If Michelangelo had put you in Heaven, I might have been able to do something for you, but down below I have no power ». Daniele da Volterra, known in history as « Braghettone » who used so much canvas to cover heroic nudes, had none for poor Minos.

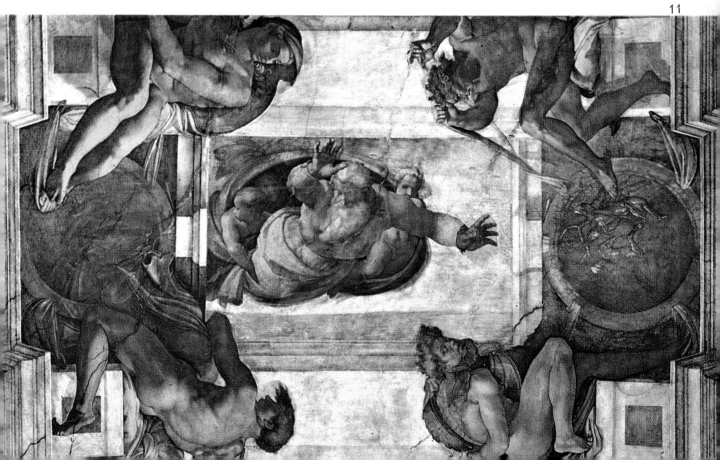

12

THE VATICAN PICTURE GALLERY

The present splendid home of the **Vatican Picture Gallery** is due to Pope Pius XI. Founded by Pius VI, it was enriched by Pius VII and Pius X.

Room I. Byzantine collection and various primitive painters.

Room II. Giotto and his school.

Here we can see the first steps of the Renaissance, beginning at Siena with Duccio and Simone Martini; at Florence with Cimabue and Giotto who lit the torch which first illuminated the sanctuary of our faith.

Room III. Fra Angelico.

The **Virgin and Angels,** a small attractive picture, was given to Pius IX by Lord Dudley in 1872. The grace of the « queen of flowers » is enchanting: against a background of golden roses the human flesh itself, seen through the diaphanous garments, seems formed of rose petals.

The **Coronation of the Virgin** is a triptych painted by Filippo Lippi in 1460 for Carlo Marzuppini, seen kneeling at the left with his hands joined.

Room IV. Melozzo da Forlì.

Here also are beautiful fragments of a large fresco painted by Melozzo in 1472 in the Basilica of the Holy Apostles. The figures of the angel musicians are full of style and poetry, comrable to the noblest productions of Titian and Correggio, half a century later.

Room V. 15th-century painters.

Room VI. Crivelli.

The **Virgin and Child** is a beautiful picture by Crivelli who liked to be called a Venetian: « Opus Caroli Crivelli Veneti » — 1482. He was a great artist, unique in his own special manner and in richness of colour.

Room VII. Perugino and the Umbrian School.

The **Resurrection,** by Perugino, was painted in 1502. The fleeing soldier is the portrait of the artist, while the soldier asleep is Raphael's, who seems to have worked with his master; in parts of this picture, the hand of Raphael is visible.

The **Coronation of the Virgin** is Pinturicchio's largest painting. Many finely painted portraits are among the figures of the Saints. The Virgin is full of tender kindness and the group is skilfully composed.

Room VIII. Raphael.

No other gallery in the world can boast of such a collection. Here, at a glance, we can follow the whole career of this artist in his brief life. He lost his father when only eleven years old. The portrait of St. Jerome, shown in room VII, is the work of his father, Giovanni Santi. The boy was still too young to have learned much from him and he was sent to Perugia to study under Perugino. In 1502 he began to work alone. His great work, the **Coronation of the Virgin,** was painted by him in 1503, at the age of

134

THE VIRGIN AND THE ANGELS (Beato Angelico). ►

nineteen, for Maddalena Oddi. It is one of his finest productions because of the exquisite grace of the angel musicians and the deep religious feeling.

The **Mysteries** painted for the altar of the Coronation, reveal his care of perspective. This picture belongs to Raphael's first period.

Towards the end of the year 1504, he made a first visit to Florence and there he studied the methods of all the great artists. At the Carmine Chapel, he learned the dramatic expression of Masaccio; from Signorelli and Michelangelo the precision of line and anatomy; from Leonardo the fineness of modelling and the delicate beauty of expression; from Fra Bartolomeo — for whom he developed a life-long friendship — nobility of composition and skilful and dignified drapery. With surprising rapidity he rid himself of the defects of the Umbrian school. This clearly appears in the **Theological Virtues,** painted in 1507 for the altar of the Deposition from the Cross in the Borghese Gallery. This belongs to the second period.

In September 1508 Raphael came to live in Rome. He freed himself from other teachers and schools to form his own. This is his third period.

In 1511, while working in his Rooms, he painted the **Madonna di Foligno.** Sigismond Conti commissioned this to fulfil a vow made to the Virgin for having protected him from a cannon ball that fell on his house, at Foligno, during the siege. It is one of his most beautiful compositions, entirely the work of his own hand.

The * **Transfiguration,** one of the most famous pictures in the world, was painted for Cardinal Giulio de' Medici, who became Clement VII, for the Narbonne Cathedral. It was unfinished when Raphael died; at his funeral it was carried behind his coffin. Part of the lower group was finished by Giulio Romano; his hard colouring can easily be recognized by comparing it with his Coronation. The lower group represents a child possessed by evil spirits brought by his parents to the Apostles to be healed. A bystander is opening a book of exorcism, but the others point upwards, as the only source of healing is Christ.

Below: sufferers imploring for help; above: active power and grace.

Room IX. Leonardo da Vinci.

St Jerome (of the first Florentine period) is a monochrome study of extraordinary power of design and expression, which displays the technique of Leonardo da Vinci. It is painted on wood and is more appreciated by artists and connoisseurs than by the public.

Room X. Titian.

In this room are: **the Madonna of St. Nicolò de Frari,** by Titian; **St. Helena,** by Paolo Veronese; **St. Bernard,** by Sebastiano del Piombo; the **Holy Family,** by Andrea del Sarto; the **Apostles Peter and Paul,** by Fra Bartolomeo and other works of 16th century artists.

Room XI. Barocci and Muziano.

The **Annunciation** and the **Rest on the Flight to Egypt** are by Barocci; the **Resurrection of Lazarus** is by Girolamo Muziano.

Room XII. Domenichino and Caravaggio.

The **Communion of St. Jerome** by Domenichino was painted for the Aracoeli Church in 1614, when the artist was thirty three years old. It has no rival for simplicity and variety of the heads, for rich drapery, exactness of the design, expression of the passions. Here the figures are beautifully disposed.

The **Descent from the Cross,** one of the most forceful paintings in this Gallery, is by Caravaggio, the great forerunner of modern painting. One of the most important paintings of Andrea Sacchi is his **St Romualdo** telling his vision to five monks of his Order.

There are other fine works by Guido Reni, Baroccio, Sassoferrato, Maratta, Guercino.

Room XIII. Maratta.

Here are: the **Madonna and Child,** by Maratta; the **Martyrdom of St. Lawrence,** by Ribera.

Room XIV. Various subjects.

Room XV. Portraits. Particularly notevorthy is the **Doge Marcello,** by Titian. Also admirable are: **Clement IX,** by C. Maratta, and **King George IV,** by Lawrence.

VILLA D'ESTE

The idea and the erection of the Villa d'Este are due to Cardinal Ippolito d'Este of Ferrara, son of the famous Lucretia Borgia and Alfonso d'Este.

Ippolito d'Este was born in 1509 his rapid and Francis I.

At the Conclave of Julius III he was appointed Governor of Tivoli, and he accepted this post although the independent and rebellious nature of the people of Tivoli made it far from desirable in the hope of being able to use it as a spring-board for his future advancement. Another important reason which induced Ippolito II to accept this position was the presence of ruins of numerous Roman villas, the fore-later, the Protector of France at the Court of most of all being the one of the Emperor Ha-brilliant ecclesiastic and diplomatic career cul-

Foto Vis-Color Pazienti

Villa d'Este - OVATO'S FOUNTAIN.

Villa d'Este - THE HUNDRED FOUNTAINS.

minated in his being appointed Cardinal and, drian, then the ones of Mecenate, Quintilius Varo, etc., which allowed him very interesting discoveries.

He took over his new office on September 9th 1550, received by the usual outburst of popular enthusiasm and by the usual deputation of leading citizens.

Accustomed as he was to the pomp and luxury of rich courts, he could not resign himself to living in the already existing Governor's residence adapted from an austere monastery; in any case it did not suit his plans.

He thus conceived the idea of building a villa in the country, which would serve as a counterpart to the grandiose palace he was building at Monte Giordano in Rome. The latter was to be used for receptions meant to foster valuable city friendships, while the former was to provide a pleasant rustic retreat suitable for longer and more carefully meditated conversations in perfect privacy.

Ippolito, in accordance with the best diplomatic traditions, thought slowly but decided rapidly, and thus the Villa d'Este came into being.

HADRIAN'S VILLA

Aelius Hadrian was the second Spaniard, after Trajan, to be Emperor of Rome. He was an intelligent administrator, restless traveller, a man without prejudices and full of imagination, an architect, a versatile genius and lover and protector of the arts. He was a mixture of the shrewdness, nomadism and sensuality of his country, and a real son of his times, the instability, tension and restlessness of which his personality reflected perfectly. He left us a clear, vivid, and indestructible picture of his soul in his famous Villa.

Hadrian's Villa is the creation of a man who strove after new things and old memories at the same time, a man imbued with egoism and curiosity. It is the fruit his experiences, nostalgia, desires and quest for the impossible. Some historians positively assert that Hadrian himself prepared the plans for his Villa and for the individual buildings which it contains,

Hadrian's Villa - THE CANOPUS.

Foto Vis-Color Pazienti

and even supervised the excution of the works. Without subscribing to such an emphatic assertion, wc must, however, acknowledge the fact that the stamp of the Emperor is visible in many buildings and that his will is omnipresent in the Villa.

To experience new delights or to relive the ones he had already enjoyed, Hadrian collected in his Villa all the most beautiful and the strangest things that he had seen in the course of his countless travels. We find here sumptuous Egyptian architecture, sublime Greek works of art, sun drenched colourful Spanish buildings, heating invented by the Nordic peoples assailed by the cold, licentious comforts of the Aegean Islands, and the latest Oriental effeminacy. Thus, the art, luxury, refinement, and variety of every country in the world sprang up amidst the solemn and peaceful Roman plain conjured up by the magic of the Emperor's multiform will.

The building of the Villa was initiated in 118 A.D. and continued uninterruptedly for twenty years until the death of the Emperor in 138 A.D.

Hadrian's Villa · THE MARITIME THEATRE.

ALPHABETICAL INDEX

Finito di stampare nel Marzo 1970
presso la Litografia LOZZI
Via T. Silvestri, 11 - ROMA